French Architecture and the English 1830–1914

In fond memory of Charlotte Ellis and
Martin Meade, who interpreted French
architecture for English visitors with
unfailing accuracy, patience and wit.

The Victorian Society
Studies in Victorian Architecture and Design
Volume Eight

French Architecture and the English 1830–1914

Edited by Andrew Saint
London · 2023

Thanks are due to the Paul Mellon Centre for
Studies in British Art for grants towards the conference
in October 2021 which preceded this publication,
and towards some photographic costs.

The Victorian Society is the champion for
Victorian and Edwardian architecture
and related arts in England and Wales.

Lectures, walks and tours are organised for
members, who also receive this journal and
The Victorian, our thrice-yearly magazine.
For information contact: The Victorian Society,
1 Priory Gardens, London W4 1TT

www.victoriansociety.org.uk

ISBN 978-0-901657-57-2
ISSN 1756-6460

Typeset in Kepler by Dale Tomlinson (after Dalrymple)
Printed and bound by GPS Colour Graphics Ltd

Front cover: The Bowes Museum, Barnard Castle.
Jules Pellechet, architect, 1869-74. [Bowes Museum]

Back cover: 'Unity' – Britain and France greet
each other across the Channel. Postcard for the
Franco-British Exhibition at White City, 1908

Frontispiece: Exeter College Chapel, Oxford.
George Gilbert Scott, architect, 1854-60.
[Wikimedia Commons]

French Architecture and the English 1830–1914

STUDIES IN VICTORIAN ARCHITECTURE & DESIGN · VOLUME 8

1 · Introduction

ANDREW SAINT

So pervasive, and so protean, was the influence of French architecture upon Victorian and Edwardian England, that the lack of any full study of the subject is a surprise.[1] From the mid-Victorian obsession with the Gothic of Normandy and the Ile de France, via the lure of Napoleon III's Paris to the love-affair with Beaux-Arts styles and methods of design after the turn of the century, French architecture is always there in the background.

Not that these matters have been entirely ignored. Henry-Russell Hitchcock's pioneering *Early Victorian Architecture in Britain* (1954) is always alert to French-ness in English buildings, seen perhaps through the lens of American openness to French influences. There are various studies of the French impact on Gothic Revival churches, while Mark Girouard's *The Victorian Country House* touches on the ebullient mid-Victorian châteaux built in England. Quite a bit has been written about the Beaux-Arts and Britain, especially as regards Scotland, with which links were firmest and earliest. But all these are partial. A wider picture seems worth trying to paint, however sketchy. Inevitably, the story is complex. Compared, say, to the influence of Italian architecture on the Victorians, the French dimension involves relations between rival and parallel cultures going beyond the realm of art and architecture.

BEFORE THE VICTORIANS

France has never been wholly absent from the consciousness of English archi-tects and patrons. Motifs and plans by Du Cerceau and Delorme trickled into Tudorbethan houses through their books. French publications about archi-tecture continued to be learnt from, cribbed from and occasionally translated.

One time when these influences surfaced quite often was the Restoration period. Wren famously visited Paris during 1665, his only known trip abroad; a few of his more ambitious compositions like the library at Trinity College, Cambridge, show a rigour that is among the notes struck by top-flight French classical archi-tects. Patrons also sometimes betrayed a liking for French styles. One such was the Duke of Montagu, who undertook several diplomatic missions to Paris. Boughton House, his country seat, and Montagu House, his Bloomsbury town house (ancestor of the British Museum) stand out from the norm as defiantly French, and indeed Montagu House was rebuilt after a fire to designs by a French architect, probably Pierre Puget. A client's personal tastes and travels often offer the simplest reason for the presence of a foreign style.

Fig 1.1. | Grand Hotel, Scarborough, from below, *c.*1870. Cuthbert Broderick, architect, 1862–7. [Historic England Archive, BB83/05608]

Generally, fashions in clothes, furnishings and interiors, also gardens, were more likely to look French than external architecture. Continental craftsmen had always been lured to London, but the Huguenot influx from the 1680s onwards enriched the taste for furnishings, textiles and *objets de vertu*. Usually there was a small time-lapse. Rococo, for instance, started in Paris a decade or so before it found its way to England under the wing of French or Flemish craftsmen. By the 1750s furniture by designers and frame-makers was suffused with French influences. But the lavish expenditure on interiors by the Bourbon kings encouraged emulation by their courtiers to a level which the constrained Hanoverians could not rival.

Between about 1750 and the French Revolution leading English architects, dissatisfied by stodgy homegrown Palladianism, started to look more closely at Parisian neoclassicism. This was the epoch of *Anglomanie*, when cultural exchanges between the countries were reciprocal and fruitful despite the frictions of the American War. An article by Robin Middleton has picked out the three English architects most pertinent to the trend.[2] First is William Chambers, of whose Somerset House it has been said that 'anyone set down in the great court ... for the first time would think himself in France'. That might be true if you were familiar with the nuances of French classicism; but the average Victorian would hardly have recognised the Frenchness of Somerset House. Then there is John Soane, personal in style yet always alert to French ideas. Soane told Royal Academy students that 'in architecture we are at least a century behind the French'.[3]

Middleton's third choice among Francophile Georgians is Henry Holland. Holland's most prestigious work was Carlton House (1784–96), for George, Prince of Wales, latterly George IV. He inherited the job from Chambers, under whom a French style may have already been fixed because of the Gallic sympathies of the Whig circle then favoured by the young Prince and his playboy-friendship with the Duc d'Orléans.[4] Holland went to Paris in 1785, and French designers and furniture-makers came in under his wing. Carlton House set the trend for state rooms in English royal palaces to look explicitly French. When after less than thirty years it was demolished, its interiors were dismantled and partly reused in George IV's reconstruction of Windsor Castle. But Carlton House was not just about interiors. Like the string of earlier aristocratic mansions along Piccadilly, it aped the Parisian *hôtel*-type by standing back from Pall Mall behind a screen. Holland's open Ionic screen, possibly based on an unbuilt plan for the Hôtel de Condé, paved the way for the festive columnar screens of Nash and Burton.

A new phase came at the end of the French wars. After a generation of hostility not unmixed with envy, the English flocked to Paris to see what had been done under Napoleon – some to copy, others to buy. Nash, for instance, ran over there in 1814, and was to crib flagrantly from Percier and Fontaine's Arc du Carrousel for the Marble Arch. At another level, Napoleon's policy of extra-mural burial, pioneered at Père Lachaise Cemetery, was overcoming its early unpopularity by the time of the Restoration. It was eventually taken up in the 'magnificent seven' cemeteries of 1833–41 around London.

As for buying, years of disruption and destruction plus the impoverishment of the old nobility brought remnants from ancient buildings and modern *boiseries* on to the Paris market, to be snapped up by dealers and collectors and stuck into English homes.[5] The craze occupies a whole chapter in John Harris's book, *Moving Rooms*. A notorious example was Highcliffe Castle, where Lord Stuart de Rothesay, twice ambassador in Paris, assembled bits of a sixteenth-century house near Rouen, choir stalls from Jumièges and Louis XV-style *boiseries* into a slapdash whole.[6]

Others took more care. At Belvoir Castle, the Duchess of Rutland installed tapestries and furniture she had bought in Paris in perhaps the earliest English example of Louis XIV revival. The ensemble was mainly put together by Matthew Cotes Wyatt. He and his brothers Benjamin and Philip made repeated visits to France and came to specialize in French-style grand interiors. John Martin Robinson lists six such palatial interiors designed between 1828 and 1837 by Benjamin Wyatt, along with Crockford's Club in St James.[7]

All these were in London. Despite Belvoir and Windsor, where Wyatville added *boiseries* salvaged from Carlton House,[8] French-style interiors were most popular in town. In the hands of decorating firms often boasting French credentials, they became standard background music for drawing rooms and ballrooms in Mayfair, Belgravia and beyond.[9] In due course Frenchness became predominant in the female domain of drawing room and boudoir, as a counterpart to French fashion in clothes and furnishings. It received a fresh boost from the Edwardian enthusiasm for all things French and by fresh imports of authentic *boiseries*.[10] In most such performances, craftsmanship and cost usually ranked higher than originality.

The first outstanding example of an English nineteenth-century country house to go thoroughly French is Wrest Park, designed in 1834–9 by the 2nd Earl de Grey

Fig 1.2. | Wrest Park, garden front, *c.*1930. [Historic England Archive, BSM01/01/104]

for himself, with limited professional assistance [Fig 1.2]. Unlike the mansions by the Wyatts, Wrest adopted the Louis XV period outside as well as in, openly borrowing from sourcebooks. A few antique French bits and pieces – leavings from Windsor Castle – were included, but most of the 'boiseries' were plaster reproductions, as often in later Victorian interiors.[11] Like Boughton, Wrest represents a private individual's personal taste, not any kind of architectural manifesto. In due course this sort of country house became more common. The most thoughtful and familiar example of the use of imported French features is Ferdinand de Rothschild's Waddesdon Manor, the subject of Michael Hall's essay below. Here a cosmopolitan client procured from Destailleur, his French architect, a robustly sixteenth-century-looking house into with were spliced eighteenth-century-looking interiors and furniture. The anachronism was far from unique. If you wanted comfort in your Victorian house, you did not have to put up with Tudor or François Premier furnishings.

THE CRAZE FOR FRENCH GOTHIC

So far, the story has been about aristocratic houses. But with France accessible once more, a wind of change began to blow from the 1820s. With ideals remote from the snob spirit of the Wyatts and their clients, English antiquarians started to interest themselves in French Romanesque and, more especially, Gothic buildings, chiefly churches. Studying and recording generally came before borrowing. In particular, there was renewed curiosity about the origins of the pointed arch and vault. Slowly, the old chauvinist belief that Gothic was English in origin fell back. A young clergyman, G. D. Whittington, who had run over to France during the short-lived Peace of Amiens, was the first to call that in question. But the debate was not finally settled in favour of St Denis and the Ile de France until the 1840s.[12]

A picturesque style of recording, as in Cotman and Turner's *Architectural Antiquities of Normandy* (1819–22) soon gave way to Britton, Pugin and Le Keux's *Specimens of the Architectural Antiquities of Normandy* (1825–8), with its accurate perspectives, measured drawings, and new jargon about the 'characteristics of Christian architecture'.[13] The Pugin family became central to this new direction: the draughtsman-father Augustus Charles Pugin, French-born, versatile and in touch with Paris circles, abetted by his son A. W. N. Pugin, already well-travelled as a teenager and soon to emerge as the *animateur* of the English Gothic Revival's halcyon years.

The younger Pugin's debt to French architecture is not always manifest. Timothy Brittain-Catlin thinks that some of his early designs, notably St Marie's Grange, were influenced by the romantic drawings in Charles Nodier's *Voyages pittoresques* of 1820.[14] Later, Pugin sometimes called for an English Gothic Revival founded on English precedent alone. Yet there are occasional borrowings from Normandy in his work, notably the saddleback tower of St Marie's, Rugby (1845–7). Certainly, the range of reference in his designing had an international breadth and confidence not yet emulated by his followers during his lifetime.

On the whole, scholars and connoisseurs got to the Gothic monuments of Normandy and the Ile de France before the architects. Ruskin visited several times in the 1830s before he knew Italy, usually with his parents; Whewell and Rickman went together in 1831; Robert Willis took his honeymoon tour there in 1832 en route to Italy; Parker visited Normandy in 1843. Then, in the so-called High Victorian phase of the Gothic Revival, English architects piled excitedly into Northern France, helped by the new railways. The consequences became dramatically apparent in churches all over England. It is now better appreciated that the force and vigour of these experiments after the compliant English 'EE' and 'Dec' churches of the 1840s owe as much to Normandy as to absolute originality.[15]

If most of these visits are lost to posterity, some are recorded in sketchbooks or diaries, while there were a few outstanding publications [Fig 1.3]. The same

Fig 1.3. | The François Premier staircase at Blois, from W. Eden Nesfield,
Specimens of Mediaeval Architecture, 1862

architects travelled also to the Low Countries, Germany, Italy and occasionally Spain, but France was the commonest as it was the closest destination. As Alexandrina Buchanan's essay reminds us, George Gilbert Scott told his student audiences at the Royal Academy to 'begin with France' when they went abroad. He also claimed to be the first to study French Gothic architecture 'in detail in any practical way'. He was there in 1847, frequently in the 1850s, and again in 1862; the illuminating diary of this last tour has been published by Gavin Stamp.[16] Burges made his first foreign foray to France in 1849, returning almost every subsequent year up to 1856 to revel in 'the glories of early French'.[17]

Street, better known for his explorations of Italian and Spanish Gothic, was in France at least four times during the decade. For T. G. Jackson, a first brief visit to Normandy in 1855 was 'a critical incident in my life', awakening 'the passion for drawing which had somehow gone to sleep since my school-days' and pitching him into an architectural career.[18] For a moment it looked as though these intensive tours were to bear practical fruit in France too, when Burges and Clutton won the Lille Cathedral competition in 1856, but French honour denied them the prize of building their design. For some architects these avid bachelor-trips, far from the sedate family progress of the Ruskins, became addictive. In 1873, William White could not start a new church until he was back from his annual continental tour.[19] Even after the craze for French Gothic fell away, its lessons lingered on, often in better-digested form, as in the spacious and gracious later churches of J. L. Pearson.

ENGLAND AND THE SECOND EMPIRE

The 1850s was decisive in other ways too. Official Anglo-French relations warmed up for a while, foreshadowing the Edwardian Entente Cordiale.

There was a political background. Napoleon III seized absolute power in 1851 through a coup d'état – 'the Eighteenth Brumaire of Louis Bonaparte', as Marx derided it in a famous pamphlet, referring to his uncle the first Napoleon's likewise unconstitutional action back in 1799. Queen Victoria was not pleased. She and Albert had enjoyed warm relations with Louis-Philippe, the King of the French during the 'July Monarchy' between 1830 and 1848. The persistent junior Bonaparte had several times tried to overthrow Louis-Philippe's régime. That led to bouts of exile in England, the last after escaping in 1846 from imprisonment in the fortress of Ham dressed as a carpenter, and to an interest on his part in British industrial and economic advances. He bounced back in France as 'Prince President' during the aftermath of Louis-Philippe's overthrow in 1848. A few months before his coup d'état, Bonaparte came over to see the Great Exhibition. Snubbed by the authorities, he had to tour the exhibition as a private individual.

But reasons of state prevailed. In 1853 the Crimean War broke out, in which the French and the British found themselves uneasy allies against the Russian Bear. The two nations now had to be friends. Napoleon III, as he now was, had just married the charming young Eugénie de Montijo. Always impulsive, he talked about going to take command in the Crimea. Palmerston, the Prime Minister, thought that was a bad idea, so he persuaded the Queen, against her own first inclinations, to distract him by inviting Napoleon and Eugénie over to England.

To everyone's surprise the two couples got on famously. The visit, in April 1855, was a great success and had wide repercussions.[20] Victoria and Albert were quickly invited back to France to visit the 1855 Exposition, which Napoleon and his Government tried to make one better than the Crystal Palace. Under Napoleon's stage management, they had a wonderful time. For their son and heir, Albert Edward, aged 13, this marked the start of a lifelong love-affair with France [Fig 1.4]. The friendship between the families outlasted Prince Albert's death, the cooling of Anglo-French relations in the 1860s and the defeat and abdication of Napoleon III in the Franco-Prussian War, followed by his flight to England and death in 1873. Thereafter Victoria was saddled with Eugénie living less than twenty miles away from Windsor at Farnborough.

Fig 1.4. | E. M. Ward, *Queen Victoria visiting the Tomb of Napoleon I at the Invalides*, 24 August 1855. Left of centre, the Queen and Napoleon III. To the right, Prince Albert with the Empress Eugénie. Right of centre, the young and contemplative Prince Albert Edward with a plaid on his shoulder. [Royal Collection Trust]

From the 1850s onwards there was a much wider dissemination of French influences in English architecture. To take an example touched on in Gilles Maury's essay, it can hardly be a coincidence that soon after the royal exchanges of 1855, Anthony Salvin was appointed to give Windsor Castle a more authentic mediaeval outline, and later likewise to do the same at the Tower of London. Salvin saw Viollet-le-Duc's first drawings for restoring the *enceinte* at Carcassonne at the Paris Exposition that same year, while in April 1857 his nephew and sometime assistant Nesfield was copying Viollet-le-Duc drawings of detail, probably in Paris.[21]

The phenomenon of French architects building in Victorian England takes off from about this time. That is the subject of five of the essays that follow – by Michael Hall, Howard Coutts, James Edgar, Joseph Specklin and Peter Howell. They range from works by Destailleur for the Rothschilds at Waddesdon and the exiled Empress Eugénie at Farnborough, through a miscellany of other houses and a grand museum, to monasteries built for communities fleeing French anti-clericalism.

There is serendipity to all this. But some patterns emerge. At the Bowes Museum, at Château Impney and again at Henry Thomas Hope's lost house in Piccadilly, there is the thread of rich Englishmen bringing back wives or mistresses from Paris. Did they choose French architects to amuse or console their consorts? Not always. Stephen Lyne-Stephens, for instance, imported the ballet dancer Pauline Duvernay and built one of William Burn's more unforgiving houses, Lynford Hall in Norfolk. After his death she lavished his money on building the costly Our Lady of English Martyrs Catholic Church in Cambridge.

By no means all English projects by Frenchmen are covered here. One such, revealed in a recent book, was an unbuilt design for Cardinal Newman's Oratory Church in Birmingham.[22] Joseph-Louis Duc – different from Viollet-le-Duc – was a high-class architect whose best-known building is the Palais de Justice in Paris. Dating from 1851 and apparently Duc's only church design, it is in the Lombardic style which rumbles around on the margins of Victorian church architecture [Fig 1.5]. Like many Catholic priests and patrons, Newman stood out against the Gothic Revival. France and Italy were the obvious places to look for alternatives.

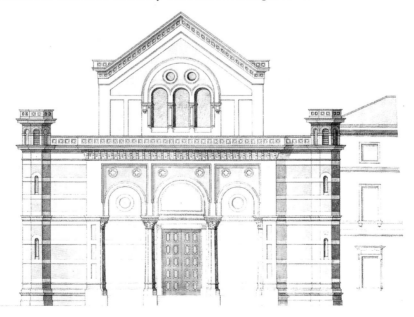

Fig 1.5. | Elevation of proposed Birmingham oratory church for J. H. Newman.
Joseph-Louis Duc, architect, 1851. [Birmingham Oratory]

One intriguing figure active in England was Hector Horeau (1801–72).[23] Horeau belongs to the other end of the spectrum from the scholarly Destailleur. Something of a wild man in French architecture, he seems to have swung between London and Paris during the 1850s. Left-wing politics may have had something to do with his initial stay, since he was later imprisoned in France after taking part in the Commune. Charles Horeau, a businessman living for a time in Marylebone, was probably a relation.[24]

Horeau saw himself as something of a prophet. His penchant from youth onwards was for large-scale urban or utopian projects. After the usual Beaux-Arts training and travel in the Middle East, he drew notice in the 1840s with designs for new market halls and an opera house for Paris which foreshadowed the *grands projets* of the Second Empire. His moment in the sun came when his design for the Crystal Palace was awarded one of only two first prizes in the competition of 1850.[25] Its striking pitched iron roof, though perhaps unbuildable in its submitted form, may have influenced the profile of Hittorff's Gare du Nord, while later on Horeau claimed that Barlow's St Pancras Station roof was cribbed from him.

Shortly after his Crystal Palace entry, Horeau came up with a weird design for an iron canopy to be clapped on the centre of one of the London bridges ('*celui de Wauxhall ou de Westminster*', the surviving drawing says on the back); it was to carry a statue of Sir Robert Peel, who had died that summer.[26] Back in Paris, he next promoted a scheme to put before Napoleon, as yet only Prince President, a rival to the Great Exhibition in the form of a series of '*fêtes*' along the Champs Elysées, '*offertes à toutes les nations du globe*'.[27] Though rejected, it was a precursor of the 1855 Exposition. Horeau was back at the end of 1851 with a fantasy project for a Channel Tunnel, or rather not a tunnel but a submarine railway inspired by the recently completed underwater telegraph cables between France and England. It featured parallel tubes along the seabed, with giant moored ventilation towers rearing out of the water at intervals [Fig 1.6].[28]

Fig 1.6. | Scheme by Hector Horeau for a Channel crossing by means of submarine tunnels and ventilation towers. [*Illustrated London News*, 22 November 1851]

Undaunted, Horeau produced further such projects. One was presented in 1856 as 'Schemes and sketches for rendering London and its environs more salubrious and more agreeable',[29] then matured and exhibited briefly in 1859. Press reactions to Horeau's drawings and models (which seem not to survive) mixed praise and sarcasm. The *City Press* noted 'Bird's-eye view, showing the general railway station in Surrey (Surrey is a large place); the new Civilisation-bridge' etc. Waterloo Bridge was to be renamed, 'as it is derogatory to any nation, claiming the front rank in the march of civilisation, to perpetuate the remembrance of human slaughter'.[30] There was a final fantasy of 1859 for covering over the boulevards near the Tuileries with sets of Horeau's big iron roofs.

In fact Horeau did build a little in England. There was The Poplars, a butterfly-plan house at Primrose Hill. The client was Alexandre Devaux, a London-based banker and associate of Charles Horeau. *The Builder* published it [Fig 1.7], noting terracotta and majolica details, and trying to be courteous about its 'pleasing novelty'.[31] Then there was Pippingford Park, a Sussex house in a bald, brutalist style [Fig 1.8] – also almost all now demolished. Here the client was John Mortimer, who had made money in the silver trade. By 1862, not so long after it was finished,

Fig 1.7. | House at Avenue Road, Primrose Hill, later The Poplars, designed by Hector Horeau for Alexandre Devaux. Demolished *c*.1939. [*The Builder*, 26 February 1859]

Fig 1.8. | Pippingford Park, Sussex. Hector Horeau, architect, *c*.1860, in *le style rageur*, otherwise 'rogue architecture'. Demolished. [Historic England Archive, BB85/3636]

a builder reported of Pippingford: 'The house was almost uninhabitable; it was not water-tight, and was falling down in some parts. Only a portion of the house was occupied.'[32] Perhaps Horeau can qualify as an honorary French member of the club of Victorian 'rogue architects'.

DONALDSON, SPIERS AND ARCHITECTURAL EDUCATION

Building abroad is always tricky, and the question arises how in those projects which were realized the French architects managed the procurement, including long-distance relations with their clients. As today, there was usually a home-grown architect or surveyor to mediate. Joseph Specklin and James Edgar touch on two such figures, both crucial to Anglo-French architectural relations from the 1830s onwards. Neither is well-known today, but both enjoyed respect in their time, and their names come up often in the essays that follow.

The first is Thomas Leverton Donaldson, who seconded Charles Dusillion on the house for H. T. Hope in Piccadilly. Pre-Victorian in taste and training (when he died in 1885 *The Builder* called him 'the last of the old gods'), Donaldson was 'a generous and fair-minded man' and an internationalist.[33] He often introduced leading French architects to the RIBA or read papers about them when they died. It was probably due to Donaldson that six French architects were awarded the RIBA Gold Medal during his lifetime. César Daly, the half-English editor of the influential *Revue générale de l'architecture*, was a friend. Donaldson also helped kick off the teaching of architecture in English universities, as the first professor of the subject at University College, London. Architectural education was one of the issues which divided France from England, with Donaldson and others calling for a more systematic approach.

The other personality is Richard Phené Spiers, who helped Henri Tronquois out at Château Impney. Spiers was among the first Englishmen to go to Paris and attend the Ecole des Beaux-Arts in the 1860s, where he was attached to the Atelier Questel. Back in London he became more of a teacher than a practising architect, as the drawing master for architectural pupils at the Royal Academy schools. Through Spiers, the idea slowly percolated that French methods of teaching and presentation were the best.

Some brief background about the Beaux-Arts educational system may help to supplement Antonio Brucculeri's essay. As its name implies, the Paris Ecole was always art-orientated, with architecture just one of three divisions alongside painting and sculpture. Opinions differ as to whether it taught about structure, materials and the business of architecture adequately. The lecturing was minimal. People attended for the studio teaching, which wasn't part of the formal course at all. Students registered for the studio of a particular master, and studio loyalty and cohesion were all-important. Foreigners had been admitted to the Beaux-Arts from at least 1850. Americans went in growing numbers from Richard Morris Hunt onwards; Scots went too, notably the great John James Burnet, but the English seldom before 1890. The favourite studio for English-speakers was that of Jean-Louis Pascal, who knew the language well, was a friend of Spiers, and received the RIBA's Gold Medal late in his career, in 1914.

Naturally you didn't need a French architect to build a French-looking house. Mark Girouard's *The Victorian Country House* lists a range of such places designed by Englishmen. Most date from the 1850s to the 1870s, in other words the Second Empire period and just after. Despite their many differences, they usually signal their Frenchness by means of high roofs, so satisfying the insatiable Victorian appetite for silhouette.

Girouard covers this disparate group of houses in an omnium-gatherum chapter called 'The Nouveau-Riche Style'.[34] The nouveaux-riches often get it in the neck for quirks of architectural style. In fact some were created for the aristocracy, like the early Wrest Park, Waterhouse's Eaton Hall or, in London, Matthew Digby Wyatt's Alford House and William Burn's Montagu House (the third London house of that name, overlooking the Thames). Others were for the gentry, like Paxton and Stokes's Battlesden Park [Fig 1.9]. Wrest apart, all of these houses have

vanished, not much lamented. Bankers and businessmen were certainly also among the clients for French-looking compositions like Clutton's Minley Manor [Fig 1.10], dismissed by Girouard as an exercise in 'aggressive anarchy'.[35]

Though these houses range across the gamut of French styles, most rely on sixteenth or seventeenth-century precedents, and often on the Loire châteaux, easily accessible by the mid-Victorian years. Burn's Montagu House, built for the Duke of Buccleuch in 1859–62, was described as 'in the Franco-Italian style, with those tall, steep roofs

Fig 1.9. | Battlesden House, Bedfordshire. G. H. Stokes, architect, 1860–4. Demolished. [Historic England Archive, BB84/1179]

which may often be seen in the châteaux of some provinces of France and which have been imitated in the Louvre and elsewhere in modern times'.[36] Sometimes the 'mansard' roofs are plonked clumsily on a Gothic or Tudor body to supply the desired silhouette, as at Eaton, not perhaps one of Waterhouse's finest moments. In other houses, like E. M. Barry's Wykehurst Place, in a costly stone-fronted Renaissance idiom for the bibliophile and connoisseur Henry Huth [Fig 1.11], there is better integration. Girouard seems to grudge its admitted qualities.[37] Edward Barry, an accomplished architect who died at fifty, was highly competent in French styles, as his fine Temple Gardens facing Victoria Embankment in London confirms. The thrusting French tower on Halifax Town Hall (1861–3), nominally by his father Sir Charles Barry, can also be attributed to the son.

Fig 1.10. | Minley Manor, Hampshire, in 1897. Henry Clutton, architect, 1858–62 with later alterations by George Devey. [Historic England Archive, BL14482]

Fig 1.11. | Wykehurst Place, Sussex, perspective of front and ground-floor plan. E. M. Barry, architect, 1873–5. [*Building News*, 5 March 1875]

Was there a group of mid-Victorians keen to promote French styles? Perhaps not. But there was a loose network of established architects centred on the RIBA, then mainly a club for discussions, that was anti-Gothic at heart and receptive to French ideas. Donaldson was at their centre, while older architects of standing like Charles Barry and C. R. Cockerell also belonged. Barry senior and Cockerell senior were both respected in France and acted as jurors at the 1855 Exhibition. Cockerell's early Victorian buildings like the Ashmolean Museum show French tendencies, present also in the work of his underrated son, F. P. Cockerell, and of the younger Barrys. Matthew Digby Wyatt, architect of Alford House, also fits into this circle. Meanwhile, George Godwin kept everyone *au courant* by publishing no less than 419 illustrations of French subjects, old and new, in the pages of *The Builder* between 1843 and 1883.[38]

Too much should not be made of this. The point is that the Gothic Revival dogmatists did not have things all their own way. Their fervent crusade was not so widely shared, especially after the 1860s. It had no true equivalent in France, where the relationship between the Catholic Church and architects was weaker. There, an agnostic like Viollet-le-Duc could take charge of major church restorations and be paid for it by the State.[39]

French influences were more consistent in urban architecture. There had long been French-looking or French-designed shops in the West End of London, an offshoot from the dominance of French fashions.[40] The first Victorian building-type to go explicitly French was the railway hotel. The whole concept of the grand hotel – a shift from its old meaning of an aristocratic town house – was French. The premier French-looking hotel in England is Cuthbert Brodrick's Grand Hotel at Scarborough of the 1860s, 'the climax of English Second Empire' in Henry-Russell Hitchcock's words [Fig 1.1]. A lover of all things French, Brodrick retired to a Paris suburb in 1870.[41]

Before Scarborough come a spate of London railway hotels. The first was at Paddington, by P. C. Hardwick (1851–4). Now stripped back, it was always a fairly standard Anglo-Italianate job with French knobs on top – end turrets, angled 'mansard' roofs and cresting. It was designed before Lefuel's large additions of 1853–7 to the Louvre, which are usually regarded as the prime source for the urban Second Empire style. Later railway hotels took full advantage of the 'New Louvre'. Edward Barry built two, at Cannon Street (destroyed) and Charing Cross (mauled along the crucial roofline). Fullest-blooded was the Grosvenor Hotel at Victoria, by J. T. Knowles, another known Francophile.

Next to the Grosvenor Hotel are the ranges of Grosvenor Gardens, designed in the mid-1860s by Thomas Cundy III and again essentially just the familiar London house-range with extra height, ornament and colour, though the development did contain one early block of flats. Cundy designed some other such ranges. and there are later developments of the same style in Kensington. Francophile architects after 1900 would certainly have turned their noses up at this kind of thing. If they are ponderous, so too are many of the Paris boulevard blocks of the Second Empire, only the latter tend to have richer and livelier enrichments.

Flats start to make inroads in London from about 1880. The horizontal way of bourgeois living spreads across from Paris, and rapidly becomes fashionable. Generally, the plans of Paris apartment blocks were taken up before the elevations. There were source books for this sort of thing; Sydney Perks in his book on flats cites Calliat's *Parallèle des maisons de Paris*, published back in 1850.[42] London 'mansion flats' of the 1880s and '90s vary in elevation but sometimes affect the Second Empire look, as in the assertively silhouetted Whitehall Court block of 1884–90 by Archer and Green along the Embankment. Greater suavity came in after 1900, notably in the hands of Frank Verity, who had attended Pascal's atelier. Verity specialized in solid, stone-faced blocks of flats for the wealthy which Stuart Gray identified as deriving from the '*appartements* of the Champs Elysées'.[43]

In the sphere of public buildings and institutions, there were several high-roofed entries for the Government Offices competition of 1856–7, notably again one by Edward Barry. Liverpool, always faithful to classicism in its civic architecture, boasted two big 1860s efforts in this idiom, Weightman and Robson's Municipal Buildings, and T. H. Wyatt's Liverpool Exchange (demolished), drawings for which were shown at the Paris 1878 Exhibition.

The ultimate French-style institution was Royal Holloway College near Egham (1879–87), designed by W. H. Crossland for the pill manufacturer Thomas Holloway – a nouveau-riche client in spades. This was Crossland's second monumental building for Holloway, following on from his Flemish-Gothic Holloway Sanatorium.

Fig 1.12. | Royal Holloway College, the main court in 1979. W. H. Crossland, architect, 1879–86. [Historic England Archive, DD000098]

According to Crossland, Holloway first suggested a similar style, but

> it appeared to me that a return either to the purer classical styles or to the Renaissance of the 16th century was certainly impending. [This was back in 1873.] When, therefore, Mr Holloway invited me to submit to him illustrations of such ancient buildings as I thought suitable in style and character for the proposed College, I selected views of chateaux in the valley of the Loire, as well as that of Fontainebleau: and these I submitted, placing Chambord first.

So Crossland was sent off to measure Chambord, where Holloway later joined him. Together they visited other châteaux, and on the way home Holloway bought for Crossland 'French books suitable for his profession' in Paris.[44]

Chambord is already French Renaissance on steroids. By the time Crossland had translated it into bright red brickwork and added undulations, intensifications and sheer extent, Royal Holloway College was wildly over the top [Fig 1.12]. It was also outdated by the time it was finished. When Norman Shaw was planning Bryanston around 1890, it is thought that he looked at a later and quieter Loire château, Menars; if so, he suppressed its high French roofline in favour of a lower English profile.

OLDWAY

From around the time of Bryanston onwards, the robustness of Second Empire styles or, for that matter, the French originals from which they derived, fell from favour in England, to be replaced by a penchant for the architectural idioms of Louis XV and XVI and even the Empire. These came to be identified, not altogether correctly, as the core of the Beaux-Arts style.

A curious example of the change in taste is supplied by Oldway Mansion in the Devon resort of Paignton.[45] The original Oldway was built for the sewing-machine king Isaac Singer, whose complicated love-life had forced him out of America to Paris, where he acquired a new French wife. The Franco-Prussian War forced the family over to England. In 1872 they settled at balmy Paignton, where Singer employed a young local architect, George Bridgman, to build him a

Fig 1.13. | Oldway Mansion, Paignton, photograph of about 1910 showing fronts added for Paris Singer by Achille Duchène to George Bridgman's house of the 1870s. [Torbay Library Services]

house, dispatching him to Paris for inspiration. The upshot was a large, Anglo-French brick villa of mid-Victorian type, less interesting than the extensive conservatories and remarkable circular 'stabling and exercising pavilion' adjacent.

Isaac did not live long to enjoy his house, dying in 1875. After legal battles his playboy son Paris Singer, best-known as the lover of Isadora Duncan, inherited Oldway. In 1897 he brought in the well-known French landscapist Achille Duchêne to remake the gardens in the style of Versailles, where he had been restoring the Petit Trianon and its surroundings. Duchêne was called back in 1904–10 to disguise Bridgman's elevations in a trumpery Beaux-Arts style [Fig 1.13]. Only two fronts were completed, so that Bridgman's brickwork is visible round the corner from the pompous colonnaded front. The interiors were no less grand, centred upon a replica of Charles Le Brun's staircase at Versailles and dominated by the second version of David's enormous Coronation of Napoleon, which Paris Singer had purchased in 1898. He hardly lived in Oldway; Isadora disliked it, and its subsequent use has been as a hospital and civic uses. Today this outlandish creation, including Bridgman's exercise rotunda, is looking for millions to restore it as well as a new use.

REACTION, THEN TRIUMPH

Generally the 1890s represented an interlude, when French influences were held at bay and national or regional vernacular languages all over Europe moved from the attractions of charm to the status of dogma. Englishness became *de rigueur* for houses in the countryside and suburbs, while variants of Queen Anne and later the so-called Wrennaissance tried to stem the French tide in the cities. Efforts were also made, led by Owen Fleming at the Architectural Association, to devise a kind of homegrown, Arts and Crafts architectural curriculum.

The Arts and Crafts Movement upheld the faith that good, honest design in any medium ought to be homegrown, in other words founded on national and local traditions and experience. These dogmas kept their force into the new century, and to an extent they survive. Among them has been the belief that the Arts and Crafts Movement was exclusively English, or at least began there. Though some other countries are now generally admitted, France has usually been excluded. This is not the place to explore the differences between the crafts revivals in the two countries, or the complex relation between the English Arts and Crafts Movement and 'continental' Art Nouveau. Suffice it to say that this reaction, this sense of difference, was ideologically strongest in the 1890s. After that, it persisted in English country architecture but less in the cities, where Arts and Crafts ideals had to compromise with modern methods of building construction and procurement.

In the unconscious background always were imperial politics. Anglo-French relations seesawed all the way through from the second half of Napoleon III's erratic rule down to the Boer War. There were some close shaves over competitive colonial policies during the 'Scramble for Africa', when hostilities were barely avoided. The last of these was the so-called Fashoda incident of 1898, a humiliation for France. Britain suffered its own countervailing embarrassments during the Boer War.

And then, quite suddenly, the British and the French buried the hatchet and signed the Entente Cordiale of 1904. Edward VII had much to do with that personally. During his reign a self-conscious amity developed between the two nations, of which the most obvious manifestation was the Franco-British Exhibition of 1908 at White City.

Architects tend to follow rather than set cultural fashions. So it may be useful to see the victory of Beaux-Arts styles over the homegrown so-called Edwardian Baroque as a manifestation of wider forces. Only from about 1910 did this take-over triumph. But the signs were there from the time of the Entente and even before, with French architects not just being employed on the odd building but following the established pattern of French decorators and basing themselves in London, as Antonio Brucculeri explains in his chapter.

Creative town planning was also at last fully embraced by the English in the Edwardian years and became a topic of fervent debate. Not all the new thinking in planning came from France, and much of what did was mediated through American architecture, now starting to be taken seriously in England, and the incipient 'City Beautiful' movement there. Germany too was a great influence. There was some tendency to regard French axial planning as wearying, inflexible and hard to integrate with the new Anglo-German layouts. Efforts to do so resulted in the unresolved centres of Letchworth, Hampstead Garden Suburb and Port Sunlight. On the other hand, the great rebuilding schemes of Edwardian London – Regent Street, Kingsway-Aldwych and The Mall are all suffused with an assured and, it may be maintained, successful Frenchness [Fig 1.14].

A REBOURS: OR, THE OTHER WAY ROUND

What about English clients and English architects working in France? Suffice it to say there were many cases. By way of a *bonne bouche*, here are a few.

My first example is pre-Victorian. Edward Cresy, a clever but not very successful architect, was invited in 1829 by a friend living in Paris to come in on an English-style speculative development in what is now the 9th Arrondissement. The idea was to build a little stucco square with a shared garden in front and private gardens behind the houses: 'Nashville, Paris', as Cresy's biographer, the late Diana Burfield, dubs it.[46] Though interrupted by the 1830 Revolution, the Square d'Orléans can still be found sweetly tucked away behind the Rue Taitbout. It attracted Alexandre Dumas *père*, Chopin and Georges Dumas among fashionable early residents. But Cresy seems to have made no money out of it.

Henry Brougham, Lord Brougham was the inventor of Cannes. Brougham was a brilliant lawyer and radical politician, but he was obsessive and demanding, so tended to alienate people. He had a romantic castle in Westmorland where he parked his wife. Going his own way, he discovered the fishing village of Cannes in about 1834, and procured designs from a local architect for a large villa there which he called the Château Eleanore in honour of his favourite daughter (sadly, she died as a teenager). Brougham never held office in Britain after Lord Melbourne

Fig 1.14. | The Aldwych, London, in 1918. In the centre, Australia House, designed by A. Marshall Mackenzie & Son, 1913–18; behind to right, General Buildings, designed by John Burnet, 1909–11. [Historic England Archive, BL24269]

replaced him as Lord Chancellor in 1835. He spent more and more time in Cannes, and to satisfy his energies had the place laid out as a town, for tourists and locals alike. He was regarded as a local benefactor. Everyone came to his funeral there in 1868 and a square was laid out in the town centre with a statue of him.[47]

Not that far from Paris is the big mansion at Ferrières, built in the 1850s for Baron James de Rothschild by Paxton and Stokes in a style adapted and de-Anglicized from Mentmore, their Buckinghamshire house for James's cousin Mayer de Rothschild. Many luxury houses were later built across southern France by English architects for lotus-eating Englishmen. One might pick out Woolsack at Mimizan in the Landes, built in 1911 for the unpleasant 2nd Duke of Westminster in a Dutch Cape style to designs by Blow and Billerey (but surely by Detmar Blow, then a crony of the Duke's).

We can end with Queen Victoria. In the last years of her life the Queen loved to go to the south of France with her unmarried daughters during the winters to stay warm, occupying a special suite in the gigantic Hotel Excelsior Regina at Cimiez outside Nice. The hotel could hardly have looked more French. Yet the interior of her suite, specially furnished for her by Messrs Waring and Gillow, could hardly have looked more Victorian and English.[48]

NOTES

1. The main exceptions are a very condensed chapter in Edward Morris, *French Art in Nineteenth-Century Britain*, 2005; and a summary by Jacqueline Banerjee of French influences on Victorian architecture on the Victorian Web: https://victorianweb.org/victorian/art/architecture/france/influence.html.

2. Robin Middleton, 'The French Connection in Eighteenth-Century England', *AA Files*, vol. 16, Autumn 1987, pp.46–56.

3. David Watkin, *Sir John Soane: Enlightenment Thought and the Royal Academy Lectures*, 1996, p.93.

4. H. M. Colvin, *A Biographical Dictionary of British Architects*, 1995 edn, p.502. The best surviving example of a house by Holland in French classical taste is Berrington Hall, Herefordshire.

5. For the furniture side of this trade, see Adriana Turpin, 'Appropriation as a Form of Nationalism? Collecting French Furniture in the Nineteenth Century', in Jan Dirk Baetens and Dries Lyna, *Art Crossing Borders*, 2019, pp.220–55.

6. John Harris, *Moving Rooms*, 2007, Chapter 4, 'England and the French Connection'.

7. John Martin Robinson, *The Wyatts*, 1979, passim.

8. Michael Hall, *Waddesdon Manor*, 2009, p.108.

9. One example was the over-the-top Louis XV drawing room at 41 Grosvenor Square, installed in a house designed by, of all architects, the ultra-English George Devey: *Survey of London*, vol.39, 1977, Plate 41A, and vol.40, 1980, p.152.

10. E.g. 66 Grosvenor Street, Mayfair: *Survey of London*, vol.40, 1980, p.53.

11. Andrew Hann and Shelley Garland, *Wrest Park*, 2011 (English Heritage guidebook); also Hall, pp.109–10.

12. Paul Frankl, *The Gothic*, 1960, pp.498–9; Simon Bradley, 'The Englishness of Gothic: Theories and Interpretations from William Gilpin to J. H. Parker', *Architectural History*, vol.45, 2002, pp.325–46.

13. This subject is best covered in Gavin Stamp, 'High Victorian Gothic and the Architecture of Normandy', *Journal of the Society of Architectural Historians*, vol.62 no. 2, 2003, pp.198–201.

14. Timothy Brittain-Catlin, 'La Normandie de Nodier, L'Angleterre de Pugin', in Martin Kew Meade, Werner Szambien and Simona Talenti (eds), *L'Architecture normande en Europe*, 2002, pp.149–54.

15. See especially Stamp, 'High Victorian Gothic' (n. 13).

16. Gavin Stamp, 'In Search of the Byzantine: George Gilbert Scott's Diary of an Architectural Tour in France in 1862', *Architectural History*, vol.46, 2003, pp.189–228.

17. J. Mordaunt Crook, *William Burges and the High Victorian Dream*, 1981 edn, pp.44–6.

18. *Recollections of Thomas Graham Jackson*, 1950, pp.34–5.

19. *Survey of London*, vol.49, 2013, p.125.

20. The cultural relations between the British and French monarchs in the 1850s were explored in an exhibition held at the Château de Compiègne in 2008 together with a book/catalogue, *Napoléon III et la reine Victoria*, 2008. They gave the original inspiration for the conference held in October 2021 and the present journal. The book contains an essay by Philippe Gresset, 'Architecture et urbanisme aux origines du Second Empire', pp.189–97, which ends with a short but stimulating summary of 'La rivalité des architectures anglaise et française au début du Second Empire'.

21. Jill Allibone, *Anthony Salvin, Pioneer of the Gothic Revival*, 1988, pp.143–6; Viollet-le-Duc tracings dated April 1857 among W. E. Nesfield drawings in RIBA Collection.

22. Guy Nicholls, *Unearthly Beauty, The Aesthetic of St John Henry Newman*, 2019.

23. Horeau is not well documented. There was an exhibition in Paris and London in 1979 with a catalogue published as *Hector Horeau 1801–1872* (*Cahiers de la recherche architecturale*, no. 3). See also David Le Lay in *Technique et Construction*, July 1979, commenting on the *Vue des plus importantes constructions élévées par l'architecte Hector Horeau depuis l'année 1826 jusqu'à celle de 1852*, a compilation made by Horeau in London in 1852 and now held in the archives of the Académie d'Architecture. For an English-language analysis of his iron designs,

see Frances H. Steiner, *French Iron Architecture*, 1984, pp.48–51.

24. For Charles Horeau, see e.g. *Morning Chronicle*, 5 Oct 1854, advertisement for French Charitable Association (Société Française de Secour), in which Alexandre Devaux also features; and for his wife, advertisements in the papers. The scheme for Horeau's submarine railway was sent in from 27 Queen Anne Street, not far from Charles Horeau's address in Mortimer Street.

25. This success has often been exaggerated by French sources into the belief that Horeau won the Crystal Palace competition.

26. RIBA Drawings Collection, SD59/2. The drawing is reproduced in *Napoléon III et la reine Victoria*, 2008, p.196.

27. The *Projet de fêtes offertes à toutes les nations du globe, par souscription nationale, présenté à M. le président de la république, dans son audience du 6 Mai, par M. M. Hector Horeau, architecte; Charles Place, ancien préfet; Ruggieri, artificier*, was trailed in *L'Illustration* for January 1851 but had been ruled out by September (*The Examiner*, 20 Sept 1851).

28. *Illustrated London News*, 22 Nov 1851; *Morning Post*, 9 Jan 1852.

29. *Atlas*, 26 Jan 1856.

30. *City Press*, 22 Jan 1859.

31. *The Builder*, 26 Feb 1859, pp.145, 155. Alexandre Devaux died in 1870. The Poplars was later altered by the architect J. M. Brydon, then became the home of Ludwig Mond. It was demolished in the 1930s.

32. *Sussex Advertiser*, 1 June 1864. Pippingford is covered in various websites and there are a few photographs in the Historic England Archives.

33. Nikolaus Pevsner, *Some Architectural Writers of the Nineteenth Century*, 1972, pp.80–4.

34. Mark Girouard, *The Victorian Country House*, 1979 edn, pp.291–302.

35. *Ibid.*, p.61.

36. *Illustrated London News*, 24 September 1864.

37. Girouard, pp.297–8.

38. Information kindly supplied by Robert Thorne from Ruth Richardson and Robert Thorne, *The Builder: Illustrations Index 1843–1883*, 1994.

39. See the study by Jean-Michel Leniaud, *Les Cathédrales au XIXe siècle: Étude du service des édifices diocésains*, 1993.

40. Henry-Russell Hitchcock, *Early Victorian Architecture in Britain*, 2 vols, 1954, illustrates a shop of 1846 in Regent Street 'by Cambon' (XII.26), and a perfumery of 1850 in Piccadilly (XII.24).

41. Derek Linstrum, *Towers and Colonnades, the Architecture of Cuthbert Brodrick*, 1999, pp.130–41.

42. Sydney Perks, *Residential Flats of all Classes*, 1905, pp.35–6.

43. A. Stuart Gray, *Edwardian Architecture*, 1985, pp.360–2.

44. For Crossland's recollections of how Royal Holloway College began, see *RIBA Transactions*, vol. 3 (new series), 1887, pp.142–3. Holloway's diary is quoted in Edward Law, 'William Henry Crossland, architect, 1835–1908, Part 3', http://homepage.eircom.net/~lawedd/WHC3.htm.

45. These paragraphs are based on Paul Hawthorne's excellent *Oldway Mansion, Historic Home of the Singer Family*, 2009.

46. Diana Burfield, *Edward Cresy, 1792–1858*, 2003, pp.63–8.

47. Rosemary Ashton, 'Henry Brougham and the Invention of Cannes', in Matthew Ingleby and Matthew P. M. Kerr, *Coastal Cultures of the Long Nineteenth Century*, 2018, pp.69–78.

48. The Hotel Regina Excelsior, dating from 1895–7, was designed mostly by Sébastien-Marcel Biasini, a fashionable Nice architect. It became the local Gestapo headquarters during the Second World War and is now flats. There is a large sculptural group in front representing girls offering flowers to Queen Victoria. For Bedford Lemere photographs of the hotel and the royal suite, see Historic England Archives website.

2 · Ferdinand Rothschild, Hippolyte Destailleur and the 'goût Rothschild'

MICHAEL HALL

On 27 July 1874 Baron Anselm von Rothschild, head of the Austrian branch of the Rothschild bank, died in Vienna at the age of seventy-one. He had inherited the role from his father, Salomon, the second in age of the five brothers – the five arrows of the Rothschild coat of arms – who in the first quarter of the nineteenth century had transformed the bank founded in the Frankfurt ghetto by their father, Mayer, into a pan-European financial power. Anselm was buried in the Jewish cemetery at Frankfurt: 'The funeral was as unpretending as if it had been that of a poor Jew', wrote *The Times*, 'The corpse was removed from the railway station in a mere carrier's van.'[1] Yet Anselm was anything but poor: he left a fortune of 50 million thalers, approximately £7.3 million at the then rate of exchange. The principal beneficiaries were his three sons, Salomon, Nathaniel and Ferdinand, and the only one of his four daughters who never married, Alice. Salomon inherited the golden handcuffs of his father's share of the family partnership, for which he would as a result have to work; he was not pleased. Nathaniel and Ferdinand made a bid for freedom by asking to liquidate their inheritances.

In 1875 the partners in the bank drew up a new agreement that deducted £8 million from their total assets of £35.5 million. Part of this was to allow Nathaniel and Ferdinand to be paid off.[2] In 1874, in anticipation of his inheritance Ferdinand borrowed £200,000 from his uncles so that he could purchase a 2,700-acre estate some nine miles north-west of Aylesbury in Buckinghamshire, which had been put up for sale by the Duke of Marlborough in May. He decided at once not to replace the main house on the estate, a fragment of a seventeenth-century mansion at Winchendon, but to build an entirely new one on a virgin site at the top of a steep treeless hill just outside the village of Waddesdon. Within only a few months he had chosen a Frenchman to be his architect, Hippolyte Destailleur, and the following year work began. The choice of site necessitated two years of laborious preparatory work levelling the ground and constructing an access road before building could start and the house was not completed until 1880, although it quickly proved too small and Destailleur designed an extension, added in 1889–91 [Fig 2.2].

Ferdinand Rothschild – who in England used the Austrian title of Baron but not the French 'de' adopted by other members of his family – recognised that he had paid a high price for an estate in poor condition that lacked a large house, but it gave him the creative opportunity of which he had been dreaming. A childless

Fig 2.1. | Ferdinand Rothschild in Renaissance dress for the Devonshire House ball, 1897. Photogravure after a photograph by Lafayette. [National Portrait Gallery]

29

Fig 2.2. | Waddesdon Manor, Buckinghamshire. The block on the far right, containing the Morning Room, was added in 1889–91. [Wikipedia Commons]

widower, he devoted the rest of his life to the building and furnishing of Waddesdon Manor, the laying out of its garden and the improvement of its estate. When he died suddenly of heart failure in 1898, his heir was his sister Alice, who owned the neighbouring estate, Eythrope. She made no changes and on her death in 1922 Waddesdon was inherited by one of her French cousins, James. He and his English wife, Dorothy, had no children, and made only modest efforts to modernise the house, the furnishings of which were augmented in 1934 when James inherited a third share of the estate of his father, Baron Edmond de Rothschild. James bequeathed the house, its contents and gardens to the National Trust in part settlement of death duties, and in 1959 following his death two years previously it was opened to the public. The estate remained in family hands and James vested the endowment not in the National Trust but in an independent trust under the chairmanship of his widow, a role that on her death passed (together with the estate) to an English cousin, Jacob, Lord Rothschild, who manages Waddesdon today on behalf of the National Trust and under whose control the endowment has been greatly increased.

This narrative of inheritance is important to understand what the visitor sees at Waddesdon today: a house that has not only survived with its principal nineteenth-century interiors intact (with later enrichments) but is also sufficiently well financed to be maintained to a standard that its creators would have recognised. As such, it is an authentic monument not only to an Anglo-French architectural collaboration of exceptional ambition but also to what has come to be known as the 'goût Rothschild' in design, collecting and furnishing. Waddesdon has been very influential in shaping modern understanding of that plutocratic taste largely because it is the only Rothschild house with its original contents that is open to the public. Partly for that reason, no attempt will be made here to describe the house or its furnishings and collections in detail, a task that has been fully carried out elsewhere.[3] Instead, this chapter will focus on the reasons for

Baron Ferdinand's choice of a French Renaissance style for the house and of a French architect to design it and will discuss his understanding of Waddesdon's place in the history of architecture, collecting and interior design. This is a subject on which he reflected in his writings, both published and unpublished, to a degree that is unusual for a nineteenth-century architectural patron and collector.

FERDINAND ROTHSCHILD

In common with all his family, Ferdinand's national identity was a complex matter. His father was German by birth, and although Anselm's working life was centred on Vienna, the prohibition on Jews owning property in the Austrian empire meant that for Ferdinand his family homes were the Grüneburg, a large villa built by his parents on the outskirts of Frankfurt; a sporting estate at Schillersdorf in Prussian Silesia (now Šilherovice in the Czech Republic); and a townhouse in Rue Laffitte, Paris. Ferdinand did not like Vienna, since he had little interest in the bank and was never close to his father, who, he recalled, had 'only a feeble interest in his children'.[4] He was by contrast devoted to his mother, Charlotte, 'the one being around whom my existence revolved'.[5] She was English, the eldest child of Nathan Mayer Rothschild, eldest of the five arrows and the founder of the English branch of the bank. Ferdinand had no happy memories of his education in Frankfurt and Vienna, but he greatly enjoyed his visits to his mother's childhood home, Gunnersbury Park, in west London. Nathan Mayer's relatively early death had left the English bank in the control of his four sons, Lionel, Anthony, Nathaniel and Mayer. They set a pattern for the family that their nephew Ferdinand would follow, firstly by their loyalty to their Jewish faith, secondly by their endogamy – all four boys married cousins, a move designed in part to maintain control over the family wealth – and, with the exception of Nathaniel, who moved to Paris to work for the French bank, all bought country estates. Three were in the Vale of Aylesbury in Buckinghamshire: Mentmore, bought by Mayer in 1850, Aston Clinton, bought a year later by Anthony, and Halton, purchased in 1853 by Lionel, who in 1872 bought Tring (just over the county border in Hertfordshire), which he gave to his eldest son, Natty, who was to be the 1st Lord Rothschild.[6] One of their motives was sport – largely excluded from hunting by antisemitism, the Rothchild brothers formed their own pack of stag hounds, and the advent of the railways meant that it was now easy to combine a career in the City with weekly or even daily jaunts to the countryside – but the principal reason was to gain the political influence essential for financiers. In 1847 Lionel became the first practising Jew to be elected to the House of Commons – as one of four MPs for the City of London – although he was not able to take up his seat until 1858, when at last it became possible to waive the requirement to swear a Christian oath.[7] All the Rothschilds' country houses were designed primarily as palaces for entertaining, and Waddesdon was no exception.

In almost every aspect of his life, Ferdinand followed family precedent. He too married a cousin, Evelina, one of Lionel's daughters, but the marriage was little more than eighteen months old when she died in 1866 giving birth to a still-born child. Once he came into his inheritance Ferdinand bought an estate in Buckinghamshire – Waddesdon was within easy reach of Aston Clinton and Mentmore – and he also pursued a political career as a Liberal, an allegiance based on the party's support for Jewish emancipation; when his cousin Natty was elevated to the Lords in 1885 he succeeded him as MP for Aylesbury. In the period between Evelina's death, in 1866, and his father's eight years later, Ferdinand had settled in England, where he led a dilettante existence, helping out in the bank when he had his arm twisted by his uncles, and, much more enjoyably, helping them track down acquisitions for the art collections for which the Rothschilds were becoming famous. Their purchases focused in particular on north European medieval and Renaissance goldsmiths' work, which had been the great passion of Ferdinand's father, Dutch seventeenth-century paintings and French decorative arts of the eighteenth century, in particular furniture and porcelain. To these shared interests Lionel added a pioneering taste for English portraits by Reynolds, Gainsborough and other artists.[8] All were to be enthusiasms of Ferdinand's.

This loyalty to family traditions makes it all the more surprising that he should have taken an independent course in his choice of architect and style for his house. The pace had been set for the Rothschilds' architectural patronage by Mentmore Towers, begun in the year of the Great Exhibition and designed by the architect of the Crystal Palace, Joseph Paxton with his architectural assistant (and from 1853 son-in-law) George Stokes, a former pupil of Gilbert Scott.[9] The Rothschilds soon developed a tendency to share architects. Stokes was employed to aggrandise Anthony's house at Aston Clinton in 1854–5, and in 1854 Baron James summoned Paxton to Paris to discuss plans for building a mansion at Ferrières, on the eastern edge of the city, that would outdo even Mentmore in scale and luxury. In 1864, perhaps because of dissatisfaction with Stokes's work on the main house, Anthony chose George Devey to design new estate cottages and other buildings at Aston Clinton, following which Mayer replaced Stokes with Devey as the architect of estate buildings at Mentmore.[10] Devey also worked at Tring for Lionel and was chosen by Ferdinand's sister Alice to remodel her house at Eythrope in 1876–9. It seems in addition to have been at her recommendation that Anselm commissioned Devey to design a dairy for Schillersdorf, completed in 1868.[11] In the same year that Ferdinand acquired the Waddesdon estate his cousin Leopold bought an estate at Ascott, also in Buckinghamshire, and commissioned Devey to remodel and enlarge the small house there. Ferdinand eschewed Devey, although his choice of an Aylesbury architect, William Taylor, for the cottages and estate buildings at Waddesdon may have been influenced by the fact that Taylor had formerly been a partner of John Durley, the builder used by Devey at Mentmore. All of these buildings were in a style that may loosely be described as Old English – Mentmore was Jacobean, with an obvious debt to Wollaton Hall, Nottingham, albeit with a central hall under a very modern glazed roof, and Paxton and Stokes's first design for Ferrières was very similar [Fig 2.3], although it was amended in a neoclassical

Fig 2.3. | Château de Ferrières, first design by Joseph Paxton and G. H. Stokes. [Musée d'Orsay]

direction after James had taken advice from the architect Antoine-Julien Hénard.[12] When in 1858 Adolphe Rothschild (a son of Carl, fourth of the five arrows and founder of the Naples branch of the bank) commissioned Paxton and Stokes to design a château at Pregny, near Geneva, the result (designed entirely by Stokes) was French and classical in style.

In an account of the creation of Waddesdon that he had printed for private circulation, Ferdinand answered the question about his choice of architect that had no doubt often been posed by his English cousins:

> It may be asked what induced me to employ foreign instead of native talent of which there was no lack at hand? My reply is, that having been greatly impressed by the ancient Chateaux of the Valois during a tour I once made in the Touraine, I determined to build my house in the same style, and considered it safer to get the designs made by a French architect who was familiar with the work, than by an English one whose knowledge and experience of the architecture of that period could be less thoroughly trusted. The French sixteenth century style, on which I had long set my heart, was particularly suitable to the surroundings of the site I had selected, and more uncommon than the Tudor, Jacobean or Adams [sic] of which the country affords so many and such unique specimens.[13]

The choice of style that led to the appointment of Destailleur was not wholly without precedent in Rothschild patronage. As has been mentioned, one common factor in the family's collecting was a love of medieval and Renaissance goldsmiths' work. Ferdinand acquired major pieces to add to the collection that he inherited from his father, which included such spectacular treasures as the Holy Thorn Reliquary made in Paris for Jean, Duc de Berry, in about 1400.[14] In 1836 this taste gave birth to an influential architectural progeny when Baron James commissioned the interior designer and stage designer Henri Duponchel to remodel his *hôtel* at 17–21 Rue Laffitte, Paris, in French Renaissance style. Its much-admired showpiece was the Salon François Premier, lined with gilded panelling carved with Renaissance ornament and inset with a set of *style Troubadour* paintings by Joseph-Nicolas-Robert Fleury of five figures from sixteenth-century European history, including Charles V, Henry VIII, Leo X and Martin Luther as well as François I.[15] The choice of these subjects, and of a sixteenth-century style for their setting, seems to have been designed both to emphasise the European scope of the Rothschilds' enterprise and to evoke the precedent of the Renaissance bankers, such as the Medici and Fuggers, who were also collectors and patrons of the arts. At around the same time James commissioned a portrait of his wife, Betty, and eldest son, Alphonse, in French Renaissance costume,[16] starting a tradition in the family that resulted, for example, in Ferdinand dressing as the sixteenth-century Casimir, Count Palatine, for the celebrated Devonshire House costume ball in 1897 [Fig 2.1].

However, the Rothschild house that Ferdinand regarded as the most important precedent for Waddesdon in terms of style was the villa built by his parents in the grounds of the Grüneburg, an estate just outside Frankfurt belonging to Amschel, the eldest of the five arrows. Completed in 1847 (and destroyed in the Second World War), the house was designed by a wholly obscure French architect named Bellanger in the style of 'the Duke of Nassau's castle at Biebrich on the Rhine', according to Ferdinand, although it was in a German Renaissance style and owed nothing to the Baroque Schloss Biebrich apart from its polychromatic combination of white walls with pink dressings.[17] He thought it was 'the first private house in that style – since then it has been copied by the score'. Equally original in Ferdinand's eyes was the style of the interiors: 'Internally it was decorated in the Louis XV manner, then an altogether new departure from the fashion of the day; an innovation, too, which was soon repeatedly imitated. My Mother had taken the idea from a Pompadour bed she had seen in Paris.'[18]

Ferdinand's choice of a French Renaissance style for Waddesdon can also be explained by the family's internal competitiveness and a desire to avoid direct comparisons being made with the great houses of the previously generation, notably Mentmore and Ferrières. A clue to his thinking is provided by a letter of 1880 to his great friend Lord Rosebery, who in 1878 had married Hannah Rothschild, the only child of Ferdinand's uncle Mayer, the builder of Mentmore, and was thinking of commissioning from Destailleur a town house for himself and his new wife:

> The Italian Renaissance requires enormous proportions. Louis XVI is the simplest and cheapest & I think as good as any for a town house. Louis XIV is grander & handsome but as my brother has just built one of that style [in Vienna] & employed Destailleur I should avoid running the risk of copying it. Louis Quinze is rather coarse & wld. not do for London I think – if you employ the frenchman I can give you several hints to prevent expense.[19]

The letter makes plain the jealous eye that Ferdinand kept on not only earlier Rothschild houses but also the projects undertaken by his brothers in Austria. Nathaniel had commissioned a Renaissance palazzo on the Theresianumgasse in Vienna from the French architect Jean Girette in 1871 and in 1876 Salomon began work on an equally magnificent house in a French neoclassical – 'Louis XIV' – style on the Heugasse, designed, doubtless on his brother's recommendation, by Destailleur.[20]

HIPPOLYTE DESTAILLEUR

Although there is no evidence that Destailleur had any links with the Rothschilds before 1874, once Ferdinand had decided on a French Renaissance style for his new house there was nothing surprising about his choice of architect. Born in 1822, Destailleur was the son of an architect, François-Hippolyte Destailleur, and an Irish mother, Eleanor O'Brien.[21] A pupil of Charles Percier, Destailleur the elder had a busy practice designing neoclassical châteaux and townhouses. His son trained at the Ecole des Beaux-Arts and on his father's death inherited both his post as architect to Ministry of Justice and a number of his patrons, including the Duc d'Orléans. The most significant precedent for Waddesdon in his career was a project begun by his father, the restoration of the sixteenth-century château at Mouchy, near Beauvais, for successive ducs de Mouchy: the profile of the much-turreted building crowning a high ridge may perhaps have influenced Ferdinand's conception of his new house. Details of the château, such as the profiles of its dormer windows, were to be reproduced at Waddesdon. Ferdinand would certainly have known the architect's two major projects for Hans Heinrich XI von Pless, a palace on Wilhelmstrasse in Vienna, and the reconstruction in 1870–6 of his enormous schloss at Pless in Silesia (now Psczyna in Poland) in a seventeenth-century French style that Ferdinand would probably have thought of as 'Louis XIV'. Pless is only thirty-five miles from the Rothschilds' schloss at Schillersdorf.

Ferdinand almost certainly chose Destailleur, however, on the basis not of his architectural works but of his publications. Destailleur's belief in the need to create a national style for nineteenth-century France based on historic precedent led him to form an unparalleled collection of books and prints illustrating the history of French architecture and design. He published influential facsimiles of historic French architectural treatises, including, in 1868, Jacque Androuet du Cerceau's *Plus Excellens Bastimens* (1576–9), which illustrates many of France's most famous Renaissance châteaux. The concept of a new national style was to be of deep significance for Destailleur's other new building in England, the imperial mausoleum at Farnborough, Hampshire, commissioned for the family of the exiled Napoleon III by his widow, the Empress Eugénie, and built in 1883–8, but was not relevant to Waddesdon, nor perhaps was it of interest to Ferdinand.[22] He was attracted to Destailleur principally because of the architect's erudite antiquarianism, which was in such strong contrast to the exuberant classicism of the Second Empire. Ferdinand thought the most celebrated Parisian building of the age, Charles Garnier's Opéra, was 'frightfully overdone'[23] and as the only contemporary English house he is recorded as having admired was Hewell Grange, Worcestershire, designed in a scholarly Elizabethan revival style by Thomas Garner for Viscount Windsor in 1883,[24] it is clear that he did not want Waddesdon to appear, at least from the outside, obviously modern. The result was a building expertly collaged from motifs that he could have seen in Destailleur's publications. As Ferdinand wrote:

> By the side of the great châteaux of the Touraine Waddesdon would appear a pigmy. The Castle of Chambord, for example, contains 450 rooms, the smallest of which would dwarf the largest of Waddesdon. But its main features are borrowed from them: its towers from Maintenon, the Château of the Duc de Noailles, and its external staircases from Blois, though the latter, which are unglazed and open to the weather, are much more ornate. Though far from being the realisation of a dream in stone and mortar like Chenonceaux. M. Destailleur's work has fairly fulfilled my expectations.[25]

In its plan, however, the house owes nothing to Renaissance precedent, with the exception perhaps of its two principal staircases, both on a circular plan. After the schloss at Schillersdorf was inherited by Ferdinand's father in 1855 it became a favourite country retreat, to which the family decamped every autumn for three months of shooting: 'It was an oasis in the wilderness', recalled Ferdinand, 'being provided with every British comfort and French luxury'.[26] His parents added lodges in an English Tudor style (their architect seems not to be recorded) and Anselm devoted himself to landscape improvements, using teams of Percheron horses imported from Normandy, an idea that his son was to imitate when creating Waddesdon's setting. In its site, crowning a hill, facing formal gardens, and overlooking an estate village, Schillersdorf clearly provided a loose template for Waddesdon, but since the house is a late-18th-century neoclassical mansion on a U-shaped plan, the closer links are not obvious [Fig 2.4]. Additional

Fig 2.4. | Schloss Schillersdorf, Czech Republic. [Wikimedia Commons]

evidence that Ferdinand had his childhood home at the forefront of his mind during the design of Waddesdon is the existence of a ground plan of Schillersdorf among Destailleur's drawings.[27] The plan, which is not in Destailleur's hand, appears to be a survey made when Salomon Rothschild bought the estate in 1842. There is no evidence that Destailleur or his father worked at Schillersdorf, so the most likely reason for him owning a drawing of its plan is that Ferdinand gave it to him as a model to be followed. The link is clear when the plan is compared to Destailleur's first proposal for Waddesdon, drawn up in 1874.[28] It was for a much larger, U-shaped house with projecting wings on the north side forming an entrance courtyard, exactly as at Schillersdorf [Fig 2.5]. Since Waddesdon was not intended for a large household, Ferdinand made Destailleur eliminate the wings, yet the house as built is still derived from Schillersdorf – both are long and shallow, with state rooms in enfilade facing across a parterre, linked by gallery-like corridors along the entrance front [Fig 2.6].

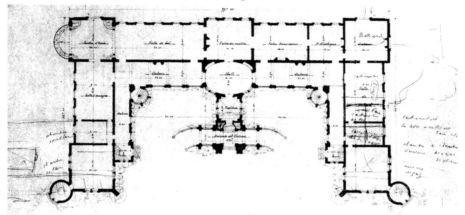

Fig 2.5. | Plan of Destailleur's first design for Waddesdon, 1874. [From a drawing formerly in the Archives Nationales]

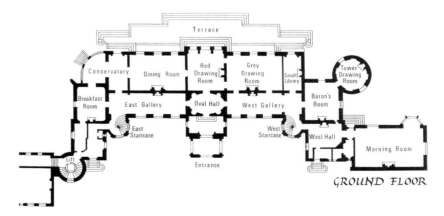

Fig 2.6. | Plan of Waddesdon Manor as built. [From Michael Hall, *Waddesdon Manor: The Biography of a Rothschild House*]

Desatilleur's first design for Waddesdon included a carriage ramp leading up to the front door, revealing that he had conceived the house being built with a basement storey, presumably to accommodate the servants, since no service wing is shown. This design has been amended in pencil, perhaps by Ferdinand, to show such a wing in the position where it was eventually built, extending from the east side of the house. Although this change has been interpreted as a reflection of the difference between English and French expectations of service accommodation, it would obviously have been absurd to have gone to the expense of excavating a deep basement when there was ample land to accommodate a separate wing. The idea of a basement can be explained by Destailleur's loyalty to his historic precedents, an aspect of his approach to design that Ferdinand occasionally found exasperating, recalling that his architect

> had not the faintest conception of the needs of a large establishment, sacrificed the most urgent household requirements to external architectural features and had the most supreme contempt for ventilation, light, air, and all internal conveniences.[29]

In aesthetic terms, however, Destailleur had a point, as it is arguably a fault of the design that the house sits too close to the ground, lacking – unlike its models – the platform that a basement would have provided.

The faint dissatisfaction that can be read between the lines of Ferdinand's account of Destailleur did not extend to the firms who were responsible for translating the designs into reality. The exterior ornamental carving was carried out by French masons under the direction of a sculptor named Doumassy, who had worked with Destailleur at Mouchy, but otherwise the building was entrusted solely to English workmen.[30] The work was supervised on site by a London architect and

Fig 2.7. | Waddesdon Manor under construction, c.1878. [Waddesdon Archive]

surveyor, Edward H. Burnell (1819–92), based in Bedford Row, London, and the main contractor was Edward Conder and Sons of Baltic Wharf, Shoreditch [Fig 2.7] – 'I have never met a more trustworthy man of business', wrote Ferdinand, who recorded his gratitude to his builder in an inscription carved on the east front of the house.[31] The demanding task of the landscaping was carried out by another London firm, George Alexander, working to instructions from a designer from Paris, Emile Lainé, almost certainly at Destailleur's recommendation – from 1876 he and Lainé were to work together on the restoration of Vaux-le-Vicomte and its gardens. Lainé had, however, been Ferdinand's second choice: he had wanted William Broderick Thomas, 'the then most eminent English landscape gardener', but he 'had declined to lay out the grounds for reasons he did not divulge' – almost certainly because he had just been commissioned by the Prince of Wales to lay out the grounds at Sandringham.[32]

INTERIOR DECORATION

One aspect of Destailleur's initial design that was preserved through the rapid sequence of revisions that preceded the digging of the foundations in 1876 was the sequence of spaces that greets visitors to the house. From the front door they pass through a rectangular vestibule, then an oval hall and from there enter a square reception room labelled 'Salon du matin' by Destailleur on his drawings, which was to become the Red Drawing Room in the house as completed. This was a sequence that derives ultimately from Parisian hôtels of the seventeenth and eighteenth centuries. One of the rooms, labelled 'Salle des curiosités', was intended for Ferdinand's collection of Renaissance goldsmiths' work and it is possible, therefore, that it was to be a Renaissance interior (as the final home for collection, the smoking room, was to be), but otherwise the interiors were from the outset intended to be eighteenth-century French in style. After Ferdinand's death he was criticised for this. According to the Daily Telegraph,

> the great defect of the house as a whole is that while the exterior successfully reproduces the features of the French Renaissance in its prime, the exquisite boiserie furniture and decorations of the interior are for the most part – and apart from a few striking exceptions – in the finest French styles of the 18th century. To enshrine the marvels of the English and French schools of painting of that period which Baron Ferdinand by degrees brought together, a later and altogether different style of French architecture would have been preferable.[33]

Ferdinand regarded such attitudes as pedantic: 'A general adoption of the art of the Renaissance, so that its feeling could pervade our everyday existence, would be out of keeping with all the essentials of modern life', he wrote; eighteenth-century furnishings, by contrast, possessed that 'adaptability which more ancient art lacks'.[34] There were plenty of earlier collectors who would have agreed – as Horace Walpole remarked of Strawberry Hill, 'I did not mean to make my house so Gothic as to exclude convenience, and modern refinements in luxury'.[35] With Destailleur Ferdinand had an architect with expertise in all post-Renaissance French styles, as demonstrated by his *magnum opus*, the two-volume *Recueil d'estampes relatives à l'ornementation des appartements au XVIe, XVIIe et XVIIIe siècles*, published in 1863 and 1871. It might have been expected therefore that Ferdinand would employ Destailleur to design the interiors of Waddesdon for him, just as, for example, Baron James had used Henri Duponchel for his Paris *hôtel*, but probably because Ferdinand thought that was a role he could fulfil himself – as proved to be the case – he used Destailleur only to design doors and some of the chimneypieces and to supply and install French eighteenth-century *boiseries*.

It is one of the persistent myths of Waddesdon that Ferdinand was able to acquire his *boiseries* because of the demolitions in Paris ordered by Napoleon III to make way for the boulevards laid out as part of Baron Haussmann's large-scale programme of urban improvements in the 1850s and 1860s. In fact, as Bruno Pons demonstrated in his 1996 catalogue of Waddesdon's panelling, all the buildings from which it was taken still stand. Destailleur's many projects in Paris brought him opportunities to acquire architectural fittings for Ferdinand. In 1859, for example, he was commissioned to build a mother house for the convent that then occupied the former Hôtel Peyrenc de Moras in the rue de Varenne, designed by Jean Aubert in 1727–8 (it is now the Musée Rodin).[36] This probably gave him the opportunity to acquire the outstanding *boiseries* from the house's *salon*, carved in 1728–32, which were divided between the Grey Drawing Room at Waddesdon and the house in Vienna designed by Destailleur for Ferdinand's brother Albert. Most of the panelling bought by Ferdinand was stripped, stained and had its ornamental detail picked out in gilding, giving the panelling, which in the eighteenth century was almost invariably painted, a nineteenth-century look. In addition,

Fig 2.8. | Grey Drawing Room, Waddesdon Manor. [Photograph Mike Fear, copyright National Trust]

the *boiseries* almost always had to be extended with new carving to bridge the difference between the scale of the urban houses from which they had been taken and the princely scale of their new home. In two rooms, however, the Grey Drawing Room [Fig 2.8] and the first-floor Green Boudoir, Ferdinand and Destailleur took a more historically accurate approach. The Grey Drawing Room is a reconstruction of the layout of the salon in the Hôtel Peyrenc de Moras (albeit given extra height, windows of a modern form and without the original over-doors) and the decision to paint the panelling grey probably reveals the knowledge that the panelling was originally painted *couleur d'eau* – bluish grey. Similarly, the small Green Boudoir was not only designed to match the scale of the room from which its panelling had been taken, the *Chambre verte* (or *Cabinet chinois*) of the Hôtel Dodun in the Rue de Richelieu, but also had its panelling of 1725–30 painted green, as it had originally been.[37] The fact that the panelling of both rooms dates from the 1720s reflects the taste for the Rococo with which Ferdinand had grown up, and is evident also in his collecting of porcelain and furniture. However, when Destailleur returned in 1889 to extend the house there are signs that Ferdinand's tastes were shifting. His decision to move his collection of medieval and Renaissance goldsmiths' work from the circular Tower Drawing Room in which it had originally been displayed into the new smoking room that formed part of the extension meant that he needed to replace the room's dismantled vitrines. For this, he chose panelling designed by Etienne-Louis Boullée in about 1773 for the main reception room of the hôtel d'Evreux at Issy, an estate to the south of Paris [Fig 2.9].[38]

Fig 2.9. | Tower Drawing Room, Waddesdon Manor. [Photograph copyright National Trust]

The choice of this neoclassical panelling, which Ferdinand bought in 1894, probably reflects developments in contemporary taste in England away from the Rococo towards the Neoclassicism of Louis XVI's reign, as was to be seen most famously in the designs of Mewès and Davis in the 1890s and 1910s.

THE *GOÛT ROTHSCHILD*

It is not known who invented the phrase '*goût Rothschild*'. It has been credited to Osbert Lancaster, although in *Homes Sweet Homes* (1939) he uses the equivalent term '*le style Rothschild*', named for the Rothschilds' now-vanished town houses in Piccadilly.[39] He defined it as a taste 'for the more lavishly gilded example of Louis Quinze furniture', pointing out that this 'fondness for the recent past' was something new since hitherto 'each succeeding generation has surveyed the styles of its predecessors with the utmost distaste'. The idea that Waddesdon is an embodiment of a taste created by the Rothschilds was shared by Ferdinand, who wrote in his memoirs:

> Whether it is to the credit of my family or not may be a matter of opinion, but the fact remains that they first revived the decoration of the eighteenth century in its purity, reconstructing their rooms out of old material, reproducing them as they had been during the reign if of the Louis, while at the same time adapting them to modern requirements. In England as yet this new departure has not struck root so deeply as on the Continent.[40]

In fact he was wrong, since an appetite for the authentic products of the *ancien régime*, including *boiseries* – for which there had been a flourishing second-hand market since the eighteenth century – was nothing new in England. There was ample precedent for buildings designed in a medieval style incorporating modern French decorative arts, as, for example, Strawberry Hill and Fonthill demonstrate. Ferdinand was presumably aware of both those precedents as he owned works that had been in the collections of Horace Walpole and William Beckford. The way that the taste for French decorative arts and interiors of the previous centuries is woven into the antiquarian revivals of the first half of the nineteenth century is a rich subject that still has much to offer researchers, but it is clear that it was in part led by the market, as dealers exploited the flood of material released onto the market by the French Revolution and the Napoleonic wars.[41] In the context of Waddesdon and the contrast between its Renaissance exterior and *dix-huitième* interiors the most telling English precursors are those that combine old English styles with 'Louis XV' French interiors in a sophisticated manner, such as Belvoir Castle, Leicestershire, as rebuilt from 1801 by James Wyatt for John Manners, 5th Duke of Rutland (although the guiding hand was that of the Duchess, Elizabeth, notably in the rococo Elizabeth Saloon, decorated by Matthew Cotes Wyatt from 1824), Windsor Castle, remodelled for George IV by Jeffry Wyatville from 1824, and Highcliffe Castle, Hampshire, rebuilt from 1830 onwards to a design by William

Donthorn for Lord Stuart de Rothesay. All incorporated imported eighteenth-century *boiseries*. It is not known whether Ferdinand ever visited the High Tory stronghold of Belvoir, although he was a friend of Violet, Marchioness of Granby (from 1906 Duchess of Rutland), but he acquired works of art that had been at Highcliffe from Lord Stuart's daughter Louisa, Countess of Waterford, and he knew Windsor well: 'the acclimatisation of French art might have been only temporary had not the Prince Regent ... settled its destiny in this country', wrote Ferdinand and he made clear his admiration of the Prince's 'exquisite taste' by giving Thomas Gainsborough's full-length 1782 portrait of the future George IV a prominent place in the Red Drawing Room at Waddesdon [Fig 2.10].[42]

Fig 2.10. | Red Drawing Room, Waddesdon Manor. [Photograph copyright National Trust]

The disjunction between Ferdinand's admiration of such patrons and his belief that the Rothschilds 'first revived the decoration of the eighteenth century in its purity' may be explained by his consciousness that Waddesdon was wholly different in meaning from such royal and aristocratic precedents. The incorporation of *ancien régime* décor into buildings that were in English medieval styles implies a triumphalist assertion of the continuation of monarchical and hereditary privilege in England, as emphasised by the customary description of Romanesque, as at Windsor and Belvoir, as 'Saxon'.[43] Ferdinand believed that such an attitude could not survive the historical forces ranged against it. Although his loyalty to the Liberals was compromised by the split in the party over home rule for Ireland in 1886, he remained philosophically a Whig, with a Whig view of history as progressive. His admiration for French architecture and design did not blind him to the fact 'we perceive beneath the brilliant veneer of art, wit and refinement, those vices of character and constitution which could only be eradicated by a supreme convulsion', as he wrote in an article published in 1888 that unfavourably compared French achievements in the eighteenth century with those of the British.[44] For him, the French Revolution had not merely been inevitable, it had also been a necessary preliminary to the attainments of the nineteenth century. In the conclusion to his book *Personal Characteristics from French History*, he wrote that the Revolution had 'swept away the rottenness and effeteness of the old order which fell to pieces like a house of cards at the first gust of the popular whirlwind. Soon all Frenchmen would be united in a common bond, animated by the same spirit, and working for the same cause, welded into one people, and developing the vast and unexplored resources of the land, not for the advantage of a limited and selfish class, but for that of the whole people'.[45]

Ferdinand had a clear sense of Waddesdon's place in history: just as his own plutocratic generation had been able to acquire estates and collections as a result of the economic and social decline of the aristocracy and the Church, so in turn would their possessions give way to democratic forces: 'Art is a small factor in history, perhaps only an incident in it', he wrote, 'yet it follows history in all its stages':

> So long as the Church and the Throne were the primary forces of civilisation it was the aim and ambition of the artist to devote his genius to the adornment of Churches and Palaces, which he filled with all that was noblest and richest in art; but when the growth of the democracy destroyed the spell of the old influences it sent the artist adrift and carried away, scattering broadcast the old artistic accumulations of centuries. A new centre of attraction has been formed on the ruins of the old, produced by the very action of the democracy. If the artist no longer gravitates towards the Prelate and the Prince, he now does homage to 'the people', whom he idealised into an entity, competing for their patronage in academies and exhibitions, while the artistic productions of the past turn to the same magnet and pass on to the hands of the People in museums.[46]

Ferdinand lived long enough to witness fears that the magnet drawing the art of the past into museums was strongest not in Europe but in America. Although the Rothschilds never set up a branch of their bank in the New World, the Francophile taste they embodied flourished there, drained, it may be thought, of any suggestion of sympathy for monarchy or aristocracy. The truth was perhaps more complex. Ferdinand was a close friend of the secretary to the American legation in London, Henry White, who was a frequent visitor to Waddesdon and may have provided introductions for the Vanderbilts and Astors who received invitations from Ferdinand. In 1883 Alva Vanderbilt and her daughter Consuelo signed the Waddesdon visitors' book.[47] Alva was the wife of W. K. Vanderbilt, whose Fifth Avenue mansion, designed by Richard Morris Hunt in 1879–82, combined a French Renaissance exterior with French eighteenth-century interior decoration and furnishings.[48] In 1895 Consuelo was married off to the 9th Duke of Marlborough – from whose father Ferdinand had purchased the Waddesdon estate – and it was on the basis of her money and influence that the Duke collected eighteenth-century French furniture of princely quality. In the 1920s – long after Consuelo had divorced him – he employed a French landscape designer, Achille Duchêne, to remodel Blenheim's gardens in a French formal style, so taking the complex story of the cross-currents between English patrons and French taste into the inter-war period, increasingly buoyed up by American money.

NOTES

1. 'The late Baron Anselm de Rothschild', *The Times*, 15 August 1874.

2. On Anselm's death, will and its consequences, see Niall Ferguson, *The World's Banker: The History of the House of Rothschild*, 1998, pp.740, 746 and 758.

3. For a detailed description of the house and its contents, see Selma Schwartz and Ulrich Leben, *The Waddesdon Companion Guide*, 6th ed., 2018. The present author's *Waddesdon: The Biography of a Rothschild House*, 3rd ed., 2012, is a history of the house and its owners. See also Mark Girouard, *A Hundred Years of Waddesdon*, 1998.

4. The Waddesdon Archive, Ferdinand Rothschild, *Memoirs*, typescript, c.1897. The chapter of the memoirs dealing with Ferdinand's collecting has been published as 'Bric-a-Brac: a Rothschild's memoir of collecting', *Apollo*, July and August 2007, pp.50–77.

5. Ferdinand Rothschild, *Memoirs*.

6. On the Rothschild houses, see the comprehensive survey by Pauline Prevost Marcilhacy, *Les Rothschild: bâtisseurs et mécènes*, 1996, and on the Rothschild's country houses and estate buildings in England, see Jill Allibone, 'Escaping the City: the Rothschilds in the Vale of Aylesbury I', *Country Life*, 16 February 1989, pp.80–3, and 'Not just grand mansions: the Rothschilds in the Vale of Aylesbury II', *Country Life*, 23 February 1989, pp.110–5. The house at Halton, designed in the style of a French château by W. R. Rogers for William Cubitt & Co., was built by Lionel's son Alfred, in 1880–3. It is now the officers' mess for RAF Halton. Aston Clinton has been demolished and Tring Park is a school for the performing arts. Mentmore is unoccupied at the time of writing and its future use is uncertain.

7. See Victor Gray and Melanie Aspey, 'Lionel Nathan de Rothschild, Baron de Rothschild in the nobility of the Austrian empire', *Oxford*

Dictionary of National Biography, 2004.

8. On the collecting by the sons of Nathan Mayer Rothschild, see the chapter by the present author's namesake, Michael Hall, 'The English Rothschilds as collectors', in Georg Heuberger, *The Rothschilds: Essays on the History of a European Family*, 1994, pp.265–86.

9. On Paxton and the Rothschilds, see Kate Colquhoun: *A Thing in Disguise: The Visionary Life of Joseph Paxton*, 2003, pp.212–3 and 239.

10. On Devey and the Rothschilds, see Jill Allibone, *George Devey Architect 1820–1886*, 1991, pp.52–9.

11. Devey's perspective drawing is illustrated *ibid.*, p.56 (Fig.29); Allibone assumed it had probably not been built.

12. See Pauline Prevost-Marcilhacy, 'James de Rothschild à Ferrières: les projets de Paxton et de Lami', *Revue de l'Art*, no.100, 1993, pp.58–73.

13. Ferdinand Rothschild, *Waddesdon* (n.d.). Known as 'The Red Book' because of its binding, this is Ferdinand's privately printed account of the building of Waddesdon illustrated with photographs. There are copies in the Waddesdon Archive and the text is published in part in Mrs James de Rothschild, *The Rothschilds at Waddesdon Manor*, 1979, pp.18–31.

14. This part of the collection was bequeathed by Ferdinand to the British Museum, London, where it is now displayed as the Waddesdon Bequest: see Dora Thornton, *A Rothschild Renaissance: Treasures from the Waddesdon Bequest*, 2015.

15. On the Salon François Premier, see David Sadighian, 'The Renaissance inside out: historical reference and financial modernity in the "Rothschild Style" interior, *c.*1820–1860', in Alina Payne and Lina Bolzoni, eds, *Revision, Revival, Return: The Renaissance in the Nineteenth Century*, 2018, pp.157–88, at pp.164–9.

16. Private collection; illustrated *ibid.*, p.168 (Fig.5).

17. Ferdinand Rothchild, *Memoirs*.

18. *Ibid.* The house is illustrated in Michael Hall, *Waddesdon Manor*, p.30.

19. Waddesdon Archive, letter from Ferdinand Rothchild to Lord Rosebery, 1880, typescript transcript of correspondence in the Rosebery papers, Dalmeny, Lothian.

20. On these houses, see Pauline Prevost-Marcilhacy, *Les Rothschild: bâtisseurs et mécènes*, 1995, pp.158–61 and 175–7.

21. See the brief outline with bibliography in Jean-Paul Midant, 'The Destailleur family' in Grove Art Online https://doi-org.lonlib.idm. oclc.org/10.1093/gao/9781884446054.article. T022444 (2003) accessed 21 August 2022. The best account of Destailleur in English is in Anthony Geraghty, *The Empress Eugénie in England: Art, Architecture, Collecting*, 2022.

22. Geraghty, pp.48–52.

23. Rothschild Archive, London, letter from Ferdinand Rothschild to Lionel de Rothschild, n.d. but 1874.

24. According to Viscount Windsor's mother-in-law, Walburga, Lady Paget, *In My Tower*, 1924, vol.II, pp.109–10.

25. Ferdinand Rothschild, *Waddesdon* ('The Red Book').

26. Ferdinand Rothschild, *Memoirs.*

27. The drawings were formerly in the Archives Nationales, Paris, but were severely damaged in a flood in 2015 and are currently inaccessible.

28. For the successive designs for Waddesdon, see Bruno Pons, *The James A. de Rothschild Bequest at Waddesdon Manor: Architecture and Panelling*, 1996, pp.35–52.

29. Ferdinand Rothschild, *Waddesdon* ('The Red Book').

30. Doumassy is a wholly obscure figure, but his contribution, with that of Destailleur, is recorded in an inscription with the date 1879 on the central pavilion of the house overlooking the garden.

31. Ferdinand Rothschild, *Waddesdon* ('The Red Book').

32. *Ibid.* On Thomas's refusal of the commission, see Brent Elliott, *Waddesdon Manor: The Garden*, 1994, p.8.

33. *Daily Telegraph*, 19 December 1898.

34. Ferdinand Rothschild, *Waddesdon* ('The Red Book').

35. Horace Walpole, *A Description of … Strawberry Hill*, London 1784, pp.i–iv.

36. On the Grey Drawing Room and its panelling, see Pons, pp.366–97.

37. On the Green Boudoir, see *ibid.*, pp.556–93.

38. *Ibid.*, pp.472–95.

39. Osbert Lancaster, 'Le Style Rothschild', *Homes Sweet Homes*, 1939, pp.38–9. See the chapter by the present author's namesake, Michael Hall, '"Le goût Rothschild": the origins and influences of a collecting style', in Inger Reist, ed., *British Models of Art and Collecting and the American Response: Reflections across the Pond*, 2014, pp.101–15.

40. Ferdinand Rothschild, 'Bric-a-Brac', p.55.

41. The role of dealers up to 1865 in what the author calls 'The Anglo-Gallic style' is analysed in Diana Davis, *The Tastemakers: British Dealers and the Anglo-Gallic Interior, 1785–1865*, 2020.

42. Ferdinand Rothschild, 'French eighteenth-century art in England', *The Nineteenth Century*, March 1892, pp.375–90, at pp.386–7.

43. On the 'Saxon' identity of Belvoir, see James Yorke, 'Belvoir Castle, Leicestershire. A Seat of the Duke of Rutland', *Country Life*, 30 June 1994, pp.62–5.

44. Ferdinand Rothschild, 'Century for century', *The Nineteenth Century*, April 1888, pp.589–602, at p.602.

45. Ferdinand Rothschild, *Personal Characteristics from French History*, London 1896, pp.263–6.

46. Ferdinand Rothschild, 'Bric-a-Brac', p.75.

47. Waddesdon Archive, Ferdinand Rothschild's visitors' book.

48. See Paul R. Baker, *Richard Morris Hunt*, 1980, pp.271–87.

3 · The Bowes Museum and Park, Barnard Castle

HOWARD COUTTS

Few visitors to the market town of Barnard Castle in County Durham will forget the château-like Bowes Museum rising above the north banks of the River Tees and looking across to the green hills of North Yorkshire [Fig 3.1]. The very incongruity of its situation and the richness of its collections have given it a fame that reaches beyond the surrounding area to lovers of art everywhere. Among architectural historians, it is known as one of a small number of buildings erected in Britain in the nineteenth century that are completely in the style of the French Renaissance, then so popular in France itself. The most famous other examples are Wrest Park, and Waddesdon Manor, Buckinghamshire – the latter like the Bowes Museum by a French architect.[1] However, the Bowes Museum is different in that no concession was made to its English setting – other than its majestic grandeur – and that it is in many ways a French museum of the nineteenth century, plopped in the middle of the English countryside, with little reference to local or national traditions.

The story begins in the eighteenth century when Mary Eleanor Bowes of Gibside and Streatlam Castle, near Barnard Castle, the last descendant of the great landowning Bowes family of County Durham, married John Lyon, 9th Earl of Strathmore, owner of Glamis Castle in Scotland. Their son, the 10th Earl of Strathmore, formed a liaison with a village girl from the nearby village of Stainton (famed in architectural circles for its stone) who gave birth to an illegitimate son, John Bowes, in London in 1811. He was fully acknowledged and later sent to Eton. The 10th Earl had tried to legitimize him by marrying his mother in a service at St George's, Hanover Square, on the day before his death in 1820. However, when the matter was tested in the courts, it was ruled that as his father had not been resident on the Scottish estates, the son could not inherit the Scottish title and estates, but he inherited a life interest in the Bowes family estates in County Durham. The title eventually passed to the 10th Earl's brother, from whom the present Bowes Lyon family are descended, including Queen Elizabeth The Queen Mother, former Patron of the Friends of The Bowes Museum.[2]

The infant John Bowes was thus a very rich man and lived the life of an English country gentleman. He was MP for South Durham in the period 1832–47 and a keen racehorse owner, winning the Derby four times. He also began a collection of old master paintings. He was active in the coal trade and formed the firm John Bowes and Partners to mine the family estates. However, he perhaps remained

Fig 3.1. | The Bowes Museum, Barnard Castle. Jules Pellechet, architect, 1869–76. [Bowes Museum]

something of an outsider in English society, and from 1832 onwards he spent increasing periods of time in France and even ran a theatre (the Théâtre des Variétés) there. He owned still-surviving houses in Paris, firstly in the Cité d'Antin and secondly in the Rue de Berlin (today the Rue de Liège). He met and married the actress Josephine Coffin-Chevallier, a talented amateur artist, and gave her as a wedding present the Château de Madame du Barry at Louveciennes, which they furnished in a lavish style; many of the pieces survive in the museum to this day. Sadly the marriage was childless, and in 1862 she sold the estate for £20,000 in order to found a museum to perpetuate their name.

The formation of the collection is outside the scope of this article,[3] but as we have seen John Bowes had already been active as collectors of pictures. In addition, Josephine Bowes was a talented amateur artist who exhibited in the Paris Salon and formed an important collection of modern French pictures. In 1863 John Bowes bought land in the Rue Blomet in the Vaugirard district of Paris and erected a picture gallery, with a curator's flat designed by the architect Auguste Pellechet, who had already worked for them at Rue de Berlin and Louveciennes. It was finished by his son Jules Pellechet (1829–1903), a pupil of Blouet and Gilbert, in late 1864. It was in the line of fire during the Siege of Paris in 1871, but fortunately survived unscathed, and remained the main repository for the Bowes's pictures until 1880.[4]

However, a much greater venture was now in hand, that of the formation of a huge museum in John Bowes' home town at Barnard Castle, Co. Durham. This was, and is, a small market town on the banks of the River Tees, dominated by the remains of the medieval castle that gives the town its name. By the mid-nineteenth century it was also semi-industrial, with numerous carpet factories along the river, whose workers lived in the narrow streets below the castle. A government report after the cholera epidemic of 1848 had commented on the crowded and insanitary conditions. This may have been one of the reasons why from 1865 onwards John Bowes set about purchasing a twenty-acre site on the eastern edge of the town in Newgate, a raised commanding site that looked across the River Tees and over to the hills of North Yorkshire. The purchases of various parcels of land needed to complete the site was finished in February 1870.[5]

However, even before that, they had commenced the building of the vast museum that bears their name. The architect was the aforementioned Jules Pellechet, responsible for finishing their picture gallery in Paris. The foundation stone was laid on 27 November 1869, and construction work began in earnest in the spring of 1870. It was carried out under the supervision of the Newcastle architect John Edward Watson, who had already designed the stables at Streatlam Castle for John Bowes in 1864. The actual construction was by a Newcastle builder, Joseph Kyle.[6] These two were responsible for interpreting the plans that Pellechet sent from Paris and creating a French building with British skills.

Frustratingly little survives to indicate the nature of the design process. Only one elevation is known, a large drawing on tracing paper signed by J. E. Watson

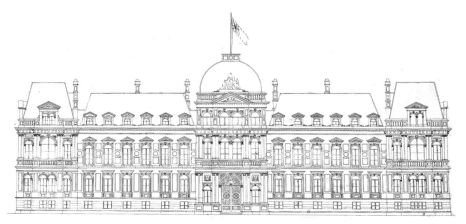

Fig 3.2. | Front elevation of the Bowes Museum, signed by John Edward Watson, November 1869, presumably on behalf of Pellechet. [Bowes Museum]

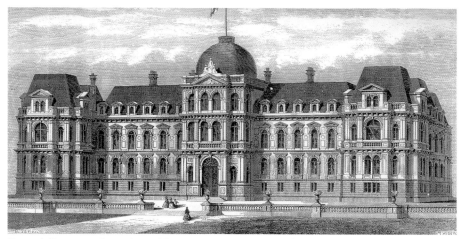

Fig 3.3. | Illustration from *The Builder*, 14 January 1871, showing 'Mrs Bowes's mansion and museum' before construction on a level surface, with the design attributed to John Edward Watson.

and dated 'November 1869', but presumably recording Pellechet's design [Fig 3.2]. It seems to be the basis for the wood engraving and report on the museum that appeared in *The Builder* for 14 January 1871 [Fig 3.3]. It shows a three-storey building of twenty-four bays with a central pavilion and two side pavilions, each crowned by a mansard-type roof. The style is completely that of French public architecture of the time.[7]

We know that John Bowes used a photograph of the Tuileries in Paris for the front arched entrance, and also requested measurements of the Town Hall in Le Havre to facilitate the design process. The estimated costs were £38,500.[8] The stone used in the construction was quarried from the local Dunhouse quarry, then owned by John Bowes, in an effort to keep costs down. The building had to contain their collections of pictures, furniture, textiles and tapestries, ceramics, as well as private apartments for Josephine, who intended to live there after John Bowes' death. There seems to have been no attempt at differentiation in the galleries, although an early report in the *Teesdale Mercury* of 10 August 1870 described the top-lit picture galleries as being based on the picture gallery in Munich, which the Bowes visited in 1868. It may be significant that the two volumes of Klenze's *Sammlung Architektonisher Entwürfe* (1869 edition) survive in the museum library to this day.

Although the elevations of the museum do not survive, we do possess a series of plans of each floor signed and dated by Watson. They show the building more or less as it is today, but with the stair indicated on the side walls of the entrance hall (July 1870) [Fig 3.4].[9] At some early date, certainly before the plan illustrated in *The Builder*, the staircase was moved to the west side of entrance hall on a horizontal axis, creating an impression of great grandeur, but possibly causing structural alterations (for instance, the pillars that support the main landing between the galleries have had to be extended with cornice-type supports) [Fig 3.5]. The only other major change in building seems to have been the raising of the mansard roof for £200, which included two visits from Jules Pellechet himself to Barnard Castle to advise on the construction.[10] Here Josephine consulted in 1871 the designer Emile Gallé, of whom she was an early patron.[11]

Sadly Josephine died on 9 February 1874, well before the work on the museum was completed, when costs had amounted to £13,600.[12] It was shortly after that we get our best contemporary description of the building. It appeared in the *Newcastle Chronicle* for 10 March 1874. It is reproduced in full here, as it is clearly written with inside knowledge (perhaps from Watson or Kyle).

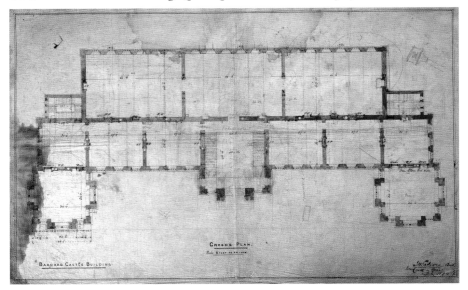

Fig 3.4. | Plan of the 'ground' floor, showing the staircase in the central entrance. Signed by John Edward Watson, July 1870. [Bowes Museum]

Fig 3.5. | Entrance hall, showing the 'bronzed plaster' of athlete by Lord Leighton bought in 1913 for £25 and later de-accessioned after the Second World War. [Bowes Museum]

THE BOWES MUSEUM AT BARNARD CASTLE

Barnard Castle is soon destined to come into the possession of one of the richest and noblest legacies that ever fell to any community. The Bowes Museum is an institution, which will probably do more in future years to bring fame and fortune to that quaint town that all its other attractions put together. The circumstances that led to the undertaking of this splendid edifice may not be generally known. Streatlam Castle, the present residence of Mr. John Bowes, is an appanage of the Strathmore family, to which Mr. Bowes belongs, and to whom it will revert in the event of that gentleman dying without issue. By his late lamented wife, the Countess of Montalbo [a courtesy title bought by John Bowes for Josephine], Mr. Bowes has had no family; and it was primarily with a view to providing a suitable residence for her, in case he predeceased her, that the building now known as the Bowes Museum was commenced. But it was intended by Mrs Bowes that the building should be so constructed as to serve the purposes of a museum and art exhibition, and it was designed from the first to become the ultimate property of the town of Barnard Castle. The death of Mrs. Bowes has entirely altered the intended disposition of events; and on its completion of the Bowes Museum will at once become the property of the town in which it is situated, subject to such conditions of administration and control, as the founder may think fit to prescribe. The Bowes Museum is perhaps, the most perfect specimen of French Renaissance style of architecture that England can produce. The centre pavilion is designed on the model of the Paris Tuileries, while the wings are after the style of the Hotel de

Ville in Havre. All the details of the building will be designed in pure French form. The site of the Museum is to the east of the town adjoining the Westwick Road. It commands a wide and beautiful prospect of every side, and extends to twenty-five acres of ground, which will be laid out in the finest style of landscape gardening. The principal front of the building looks towards the south and will be 300ft in length. On the east and west there are wings each 130ft in length, and within these wings the front is set back 38ft. The main doorway is 24ft 6in high by 12ft 6in wide, and the entrance hall is 42ft square by 31ft high. In the basement floor there are 24 rooms for the use of servants. On the ground floor there are eight rooms intended for the purposes of the Museum, and three rooms for the reception of sculpture. Above the sculpture galleries there will be a fine picture gallery 200ft by 45ft. In the upper storey there are about 50 servant's rooms. On each floor there are private reception rooms, and apartments for the use of attendants. The principal staircase is 56ft high and 32ft wide. There are 54 steps, 10 feet wide, and constructed of Aberdeen graphite. The landings of the different galleries are built of stone from the Craigleith quarries, Edinburgh, the under landings being supported by red and the upper landings by grey granite columns. There is a staircase in each landing consisting of 102 steps of Craigleith stone. The center dome of the building will be 130 feet in height, and will contain an observatory to the charge of which a competent astronomer will be appointed. The foundation stone of this magnificent edifice was laid in November, 1869, by Mrs Bowes, without any show or ceremony. It has thus been over four years in course of construction, and notwithstanding that about 120 men have been employed upon it during the whole of that time it is expected that over four years will be required to complete it. A chapel will be built in the grounds of the museum, on the model of a rather celebrated chapel that was destroyed in Paris during the siege. The chapel will accommodate between 400 and 500 worshippers, and although it is to be build primarily for the attendants and officials connected with the museum, it will be open for the use of the general public. In the grounds, which will be laid out with all the taste and resources of horticultural art, there is to be an orangery, wherein about twenty trees of great age and enormous size, will be planted. These trees belonged to the late King Louis Philippe, and were acquired by Mrs. Bowes at considerable cost. The conservatories will be constructed in a style corresponding to the other accessories of the museum. When completed, the museum will receive about 1,600 paintings – some of them very rare and valuable – which Mr and Mrs Bowes have collected over a period of years in the course of their continental travels. These paintings were stored in a house in Paris during the siege, and were in imminent danger of being destroyed – so much so, indeed, that a shell burst in the garden of the house in which they were placed for safety, and did considerable damage. A large collection of sculpture belonging to and collected by Mrs. Bowes is also waiting to be placed in the museum. It is well known that the late Countess of Montalbo had the taste and experience of an accomplished connoisseur – being herself an artist of no mean ability, so that the collection of paintings and statuary which she gathered together for the purpose of her museum are likely to provide a rare treat for our northern virtuosi. A gift of this sort is not, perhaps, to be correctly or fairly estimated by a standard of points, shilling and pence; but it may be stated that the cost of the building when completed will not be much short of £150,000.

This description tallies exactly with the main building as it exists today, except that the chapel and observatory were never finished (materials for the construction of an oak staircase existed into the 1960s) and the orangery was never constructed. The sculpture gallery, on the first floor below the picture galleries, was fitted out with a collection of casts before the First World War, but was disbanded in the 1950s, when the casts were sent up to the Fine Art Department of Newcastle University.

The park began to be laid out and landscaped at this time. It makes full use of the sloping site, which are planted with a great variety of specimen trees purchases in 1870 to 1876. A machine for lifting trees was bought from the local iron-founders, William Smith and Sons, in December 1870. The bills for planting survive in the Durham County Record Office and include ones from suppliers such as Ralph Robson, nurseryman and seedsman, Hexham (24 June 1870): John Hunter, nurseryman (30 June 1870 and October 1870), William Waistill, surveyor, Northallerton, for making plans (9 February 1872), Hunter and Robson (1871 and 13 March 1876) Little and Ballantyne, Carlisle (Knowefield, Stanwix 1874); Thomas Hunter, 13 March 1876. In all, over 4500 plants are listed.[13] Some of the trees survive today. A famous monkey puzzle tree (*auraucaria imbricata*), which was purchased for fifteen guineas on 28 July 1871 from Henry Lane and Son, Great Berkhamstead, Herts, features in many early views of the museum and died only in the last few years. This was more than the Bowes paid for their paintings by El Greco and Goya.

Behind the museum was a large pool to act as a water supply in the event of fire. In front was a large parterre below a terrace wall, which was constructed in 1878.[14] This is likely to be the date of the plan and elevation in the museum's collections showing the terrace wall with statues in the niches, presumably by Pellechet [Figs 3.6, 3.7]. However, it is not clear whether the parterre was planted in John Bowes' lifetime. The entrance lodges to the museum, also designed by Pellechet, were begun in 1880 and the gardens were finished with the basins and ponds in 1883.[15]

The major feature of the park, however, was a large Roman Catholic chapel in the Gothic style that was to be build 60 yards to the east of the museum building. This was intended to hold the remains of John and Josephine, its site being laid down in her will of July 1871. The land was conveyed to separate trustees in March 1874. It was designed by Pellechet following the style of the church of St Rémy, Vanves, south of Paris. The foundation stone of the chapel was laid by Watson and Kyle on 6 April 1875. It was to cost £35,000 and was to serve also as the Roman Catholic church for Barnard Castle. However, there were queries over access through the museum park, and John Bowes himself was in disagreement with the Roman Catholic bishop over the right to appoint the incumbent. For these reasons, as well as financial pressures, building ceased 1876 and only the outer walls were built to half-level.[16] John and Josephine were eventually buried (temporarily) in the Bowes family chapel at Gibside.

Meanwhile, work continued apace on the main body of the museum, with the roof and parquetry put down in picture galleries by French craftsmen.[17] Pellechet

Figs 3.6, 3.7. | Undated drawings in pen and wash for the terrace and parterre, attributed to Jules Pellechet. Above, plan showing excavated parterre in front of the museum, with variant design at the top. Below, elevation showing façade of the terrace facing the parterre. [Bowes Museum]

himself visited in early 1875.[18] The expenses of the museum were as much as £100,000 in 1876.[19] In 1878 the first objects were brought in, but the museum had still to be fitted out. It received its first human inhabitant in 1879, when the first curator, Robert Harley, was appointed and took up his accommodation in what were to have been Josephine's rooms on the third floor.[20]

Pellechet made a return visit in 1879, to advise on a new orangery at Streatlam Castle, and on the installation of the magnificent iron doors at the museum. These are by Bardin and Son, of Paris, who saw them off by boat from Paris on 13 February. Each door, with bronze enrichments, weighed over four tons. The showcases in the museum were also French, supplied by Haret, the French contractor who supplied cases for the Paris 1878 Exhibition, and may have been used earlier, as some of them bore name-plaques that related to the Vienna Exhibition of 1873.

A letter from John Bowes in the museum archives suggests they may even have been used in the Paris Exhibition of 1867. They cost the knockdown price of £1,600 and were sent over in kit form to be assembled on site.[21]

The total expenditure in 1879 mounted to £6,800 of which Kyle's building work was £3,000.[22] Such expenditure unfortunately coincided with diminishing coal-mining revenue towards the end of John Bowes' life. In 1883 finishing touches were put not only to the lodges and drives, but to a central heating system inside and the fine carved stonework outside. This was actually carved in situ, craftsmen working from scaffolding, following plaster models sent over from Paris at a total cost of £2,400 [Fig 3.8].[23]

In 1884, the curator, Robert Harley died, to be succeeded by Owen Scott of the South Kensington Museum.[24] J. E. Watson died the next year, to be followed soon after by John Bowes himself. In his will he left £135,000 to a body of trustees to run the museum. However, his will took many years to prove and the final sum of £142,887 18s 9d was not received until 1905, but debts had to be paid from this.[25]

In these circumstances, little major work could be done. The first trustees meeting took place at Gwydir House, Whitehall, in 1886, but finance was so tight

Fig 3.8. | Plaster maquette with entwined initials BM for Bowes/Montalbo, used for carving the central key stone above the entrance door. [Bowes Museum]

that there was little they could do other than permit the curator to continue his work of arranging specimens in the galleries. However, there were numerous requests to view the collections [Fig 3.9] and attempts were made to provide access, even though no proper balustrade existed on the main staircase and landing. In 1890 the *Teesdale Mercury* (26 February) refers to the removal of 'unsightly hoardings' and 'the situation of neat, if rather tall railings' outside the museum. The museum opened for the public officially, but on borrowed money, on 10 June 1892.[26]

Fig 3.9. | View of the picture galleries before the installation of central heating in 1905. [Bowes Museum]

The museum continued under severe financial problems, most notably in 1899, and few improvements were made. In 1901 the curator, Owen Scott, was given six months' leave of absence to organize the Fine Arts Section of the Glasgow Exhibition of that year (Trustees' Minutes of 16 October 1900). He must have used his time to get to know the Glasgow art world, and met John Keppie of Honeyman, Keppie and Mackintosh. Keppie was the most classicising of this famous partnership, and was to have an important influence on the appearance of the museum. When in 1905 payment of the final legacy was received, and gave the trustees money for further improvements, it was Keppie that selected the new designs (Minutes of 15 March 1906). A stone balustrade to the first-floor landing was commissioned from J. Kyle and Sons for £175, while the entrance gates and staircase balustrade were commissioned from the firm of J.W. Singer and Sons of Frome, Somerset at a cost of £795 and £523 15s [Fig 3.10]. Their drawings survive in the museum archive to this day.[27]

At the same time the entrance floor was paved with Hopton Wood stone and black Belgian marble by Gordon of Durham.[28]

The downside was that dry rot was found in the beams and they had to be replaced over a period of three years with steel beams to a cost of £15,000 by the Cleveland Bridge Company.[29] The museum closed in 1906 for reasons of dry rot and did not reopen until 1909, when tennis courts with a pavilion were laid out. It was at this stage that the trustees gave one of their more interesting commissions, inspired by Owen Scott's Scottish links. In December 1911 they invited John Keppie to submit a design for a bandstand in the centre of the parterre with materials of his choice. He visited in January 1912, and

Fig 3.10. | Wrought-iron main gates to the Bowes Museum, by Singer of Frome, c.1905. [Bowes Museum]

presumably supplied the beautiful watercolour design that survives in the museum shortly after [Fig 3.11]. It shows an elaborate pavilion with a dome supported on Corinthian columns in the full 'Beaux-Arts' style. However, the estimated price of £2,900 was thought too high (Trustees' minutes of October) and in March 1912 designs from other architects were sought. On 4 April 1912 Keppie asked for a fee of £50 plus expenses, but was given 40 guineas in full discharge of his time and trouble. In the same month, an amended design for an iron bandstand from Parker, Winder and Achurch of Birmingham was accepted.[30]

It was opened by Lady Glamis, daughter in law of the Earl of Strathmore, on 5 August. It survived [Fig 3.12] until 1951, when a local firm was paid £25 to take it away for scrap. Other more pragmatic additions of this year include a still-surviving hydraulic lift by Pickering of Stockton to the curator's flat, in use until 1960;[31] and the inner porch to the hall, from designs by a local architect (and caricaturist), E. C. Surtees (Trustees' Minutes of 23 March).

With the coming of the First World War the museum was requisitioned by the War Office, and little was done to the buildings. It was now entering a period of stagnation, caused by chronic lack of finance. However, the proposed Catholic church was taken in hand in the 1920s. The church trustees had received nearly £20,000 under John Bowes' will to finish this, and they obtained designs from a number of leading architects. However, disputes over access with the museum trustees led to the selection of a new site in the south-west corner of the museum park, with direct access to the road. In 1922 they commissioned Ellison Fenwicke

Fig 3.11. | Unexecuted design for a bandstand by John Keppie of Honeyman, Keppie & Mackintosh architects, Glasgow, 1912. [Bowes Museum]

Fig 3.12. | Aerial view of the Bowes Museum taken before the demolition of the bandstand in 1951.

of Dunn, Hanson and Fenwicke of Newcastle to produce a 'suitable church to accommodate not less that 350 people, and also for a priest's house with four bedrooms and other suitable accommodation'. It was built by the firm of Messrs. A. Pringle out of Stainton stone at a cost of nearly £25,000. The foundation stone was laid on 30 October 1926 and the church consecrated on 29 September 1928. Meanwhile the bodies of John and Josephine Bowes had been taken from the Bowes family vault at Gibside and reinterred outside the east end of the new church on 14 July 1928.[32]

The museum's chronic financial problems were exacerbated by the Second World War, and little new work was done other than turning over the coal vaults on the ground floor for local displays. Threats of closure and sale led to the transfer of the trusteeship to the Education Committee of Durham County Council in 1956. The museum gained a new lease of life, mostly obvious in the rearrangement of the interiors, which were set out in the form of 'period rooms' on the first floor. Emphasis began to be placed on the historic nature of the building. Some garden sculpture was brought over in the form of discarded statues from the Houses of Parliament and two heraldic beasts from the Assize Court, Manchester, now stand on the terrace opposite the main entrance. The parterre was restored in 1981 using Pellechet's designs in the museum archive. The building, collections and park remain as a unique monument to enlightened nineteenth-century philanthropy, and well merit their official status (Grade I and Grade II listed) as a rare example of a nineteenth-century scheme of collecting, planning and building surviving more or less intact to the present day.

ACKNOWLEDGEMENTS

This article is based on research carried out by Charles Hardy, Head of History at Barnard Castle School, and published in his book *John Bowes and The Bowes Museum*, 1970, based on his study of archives at the Bowes Museum (then uncatalogued); also on archives now at Durham County Record Office and other sources; an English Heritage report on the Bowes Museum 1999, and notes complied by Sarah Medlam, former Curator of Furniture.

NOTES

1. Mark Girouard, *The Victorian Country House*, 1971, pp.131–6.

2. Margaret Wills, *Gibside and the Bowes Family*, 1995.

3. For a general introduction to the museum and the history of its objects see E. Western, *A History of the Bowes Museum and Park*, 1890, and Elizabeth Conran et al., *The Bowes Museum*, 1992.

4. For this and many other references taken from then uncatalogued archive material see Charles Hardy, *John Bowes and the Bowes Museum*, 1970, p.141.

5. Hardy, pp.144, 163.

6. *Ibid.*, p.162.

7. For French museums of the nineteenth century see Chantal Georgel, *La Jeunesse des Musées: les musées de France au XIXe siècle*, Musée d'Orsay, 1994.

8. Hardy, p.161.

9. Other plans are in the Durham County Record Office (D/St/P2/9/1,2; further records are at D/Bo/E 1–41, DE/Bo/F 88,89).

10. Hardy, p.178.

11. Gabriella Gros-Galliner, 'A French Connection: Emile Gallé and the Bowes. The Gallé Correspondence at The Bowes Museum, Barnard Castle', *The Connoisseur*, Sept 1979, p.51.

12. Hardy, p.192.

13. Durham County Record Office, D/Bo/E7–27 (old numbering).

14. Hardy, p.211.

15. *Ibid.*, p.230; *Teesdale Mercury*, 9 June 1880.

16. Hardy, p. 96.

17. *Ibid.*, p.200. See also Durham County Record Office, D/St/C5/297/136, 'notes on the picture gallery ceiling sent to J E Watson', Dent to Bowes, 16 Nov 1872, with reply. John Bowes refers to the 'case with the folding doors with mirrors in them which Mrs. Bowes obtained for the entrance door of the picture gallery' in a letter of 27 December (?) 1876.

18. Hardy, p.204.

19. *Ibid.*, p.214.

20. *Ibid.*, p.212.

21. *Ibid.*, p.215. Further details on the finishing of the building survive in Durham County

Record Office, including: D/St/C5/461/2, J. T. McCulloch, architectural sculpture [for facade carvings?], 26 April 1876; D/St/C5/517/4, windows, cellars, types of marble, March 1871; D/St/C5/542/1 and 554/1-4m stoves from Spencer of Oxford Street, 16 December 1878; also Mortlock; D/St/C5/573/30, more carved work from G. S. Arrowsmith, 1882; D/St/C5/573/31, window (?) glass (?), 1882 [or for museum cabinets?]; D/St/C5/577/746, two cabinet makers, 1882 [for museum cabinets?].

22. Hardy, p.223.

23. *Ibid.,* p. 230; a letter from John Bowes of 12 September 1876 refers to the arrival of the 'plaister models'.

24. The early years of the Bowes Museum have been discussed by Simon Spier, 'Creating The Bowes Museum, *c.*1858-1917: Private Collecting and the Art Market in the Public Art Museum', PhD thesis, University of Leeds, 2021. Staffing references include Durham County Record Office, D/St/C5/309/002: 1873 [26 January], John Wilks offered job in charge of staff on site (he declined); D/St/C5/436.1: Robert Harley from Lewisham, London, applied for curatorship
5 December 1874 (and later died); D/St/C5/595/15–36: recruitment of Owen Scott, curator (the post was turned down by Hungerford Pollen).

25. Hardy, p.268.

26. *Ibid.,* p.265.

27. Though a letter to the curator of 24 August 1955, from Jane O. Shirley Elgood suggests the balustrade of the staircase and landing were made by her father, Thomas S. Elgood, of Elgood Brothers, Leicester, art metal workers.

28. Hardy, p.269.

29. *Ibid.,* p.269. One of the beams, above the old library on the ground floor, was found to be inscribed 'Mouncey 1908' in chalk [October 2008].

30. It corresponds with model no.24 or 25 from the Lion Foundry of Kirkintilloch, who record an order in 1912 'Order F1988 – a bandstand for BARNARD CASTLE' (letter from Maurice Bradbury, 6 December 2007).

31. Hardy, p. 269; Frank Atkinson, *Industrial Archaeology of North-East England, Volume 2: The Sites,* 1974, p.269.

32. D. Milburn, 'New for Old: The Bowes Museum Chapel and Park', *Northern Catholic History*, no. 34, 1993, pp.46–57, and 'Fait Accompli: The Bowes Memorial Church at Last', *ibid.*, no. 36, 1995, pp.42–57. A three-dimensional watercolour view of the church in its parkland setting, by the architects was sold at Addison's, Barnard Castle, 17 September 2005, lot 264.

4 · The Salt King's Château at Impney

JAMES EDGAR

Château Impney, or Impney Hall as it was known when constructed in the 1870s, was built for John Corbett, MP for Droitwich, to the designs of the French architect, Auguste Tronquois, with the help of Richard Phené Spiers. Nikolaus Pevsner wrote that Impney, 'it can't be denied, is thoroughly debased, yet its exuberance is catching.'[1] [Fig 4.1]

THE CLIENT

John Corbett was born at The Delph, Brierley Hill, Staffordshire, on 12 June 1817.[2] His father had moved to Staffordshire to become a carrier operating canal boats. Corbett left school at the age of 10 or 11 and then worked on the boats for the next dozen or so years. He was keenly interested in matters mechanical and, in 1840, was apprenticed for five years to William Lester, chief engineer of Messrs Hunt and Brown of the Leys Ironworks, Stourbridge. After serving his apprenticeship he left the ironworks and became a partner in the carrier firm of Corbett & Son, the main cargo for which was coal, iron and possibly salt, sailing between Lancashire, the Midlands and London.

Salt had begun to be exploited at Stoke Prior, north of Droitwich, in 1825 and two companies, producing soda, vitriol and soap in addition to salt, were established on either side of the Worcester and Birmingham Canal. Corbett had become an agent for the British Alkaline Company on the east side, and in the 1851 census he was described as a salt merchant. In 1852 the carrier business was sold, the advent of railways threatening to diminish canal traffic, and Corbett took a lease on the Stoke Prior salt works. By this date the two chemical companies were failing; one was offered for sale and the other went into liquidation in the following year. Corbett raised capital and by 1857 he had leased and purchased parts of both sites (and a warehouse in Gloucester) finally purchasing the whole outright a decade later.

The enterprises were transformed by lining new brine pits with cast-iron cylinders to prevent the inflow of fresh water that had brought contaminants. Corbett patented a system of 'improvements in evaporating pans' (1860) and by installing a system of pipes he was able to double the intensity of the heat and steam and produce a whiter, more finely grained salt than was obtainable elsewhere. Three grades of salt – renowned for purity – were offered; the lowest grade was used as agricultural fertiliser. Over the next quarter of a century production was increased from 26,000 tons to 200,000 tons per annum. New

Fig 4.1. | Château Impney, Droitwich, Worcestershire. Garden front with fountain.
[Historic England Archive, DP114135]

Fig 4.2. | Corbett's Stoke Prior saltworks on the Worcester and Birmingham Canal after rebuilding in 1871–2. [*Royal Album of Arts and Industries of Great Britain*, 1887]

works were built in 1871–2 [Fig 4.2]. Corbett travelled extensively across the globe promoting the business, and the products won numerous international awards. The company retained fifty canal boats for its own use, cutting tributaries from the canal and forming branches off the railway. It also built 500 railway wagons, and had a foundry, fitting shops, sawmills and a brickyard. There were seven depots throughout the United Kingdom and agencies throughout the Colonies. Cottages with gardens were erected for the workers and Corbett commissioned schools, lecture rooms, a club house and a dispensary.

MARRIAGE AND THE MOVE TO IMPNEY

In April 1856 Corbett married Anna Eliza, daughter of John O'Meara, of Co. Tipperary, and Elizabeth Fitzpatrick who had been born in Bordeaux. O'Meara had a role in the British Diplomatic Corps in Paris and was Secretary to the Cercle de l'Union, an exclusive club including numerous French and foreign aristocrats, politicians, bankers and the like. The marriage took place at the British Embassy. Corbett must have met his wife some time before, possibly when he visited the 1855 Exposition Universelle in Paris; the exhibition included displays of innovations in industry, including two from Droitwich's salt manufacturers, W. & J. Noak and Clay and Newman. Corbett took his bride back to England to live at Rigby Hall, a modest classical house with five principal bedrooms set in 25 acres of grounds. The house, which he had taken on a lease, was within four miles of the salt works and half a mile from Bromsgrove Station, one stop along the line from the works. The family, which eventually extended to three daughters, two sons and seven servants, continued to live in leased accommodation until Impney was completed: from 1863 until after February 1872 at The Grange, Stoke Prior, and then for a short time at Perdiswell Hall, Worcester.

Corbett's interest in social and political matters – he was a Liberal – led him to contest, unsuccessfully, the parliamentary seat for Droitwich in 1868. The prospective candidate would have been close to the local politicians, and in the same year Impney Lodge was put up for sale following the death of Thomas Thould, miller and magistrate for Droitwich. The property was bought in October 1868 on behalf of John Blick, Mayor of Droitwich, but sold soon after to Corbett.[3] The existing house was built of brick, stuccoed and slated. It had eight bedrooms, three reception rooms, a small study and all the usual service rooms, with a carriage-drive approach and tastefully laid-out pleasure grounds and lawns, planted with conifers and evergreens in great variety, coach house, stabling and kitchen garden. The estate included a farm and all the requisite buildings and a four-storey water mill on the Salwarpe, with a long leat running through the grounds.

In March 1872 Corbett bought substantial extra land to add to his new estate from the neighbouring proprietor, Earl Somers.[4] Negotiations for the purchase of this land were mostly settled in November of the preceding year with Corbett corresponding from the Hotel Mirabeau, Rue de la Paix, Paris; he eventually agreed to pay £27,200. One of the letters indicates that he was about to leave Paris and travel to Italy via the newly opened Mount Cenis tunnel and then on to Brindisi and eventually to Alexandria, Cairo and up the Nile. At this time he appears to have been going back and forth between Worcestershire and Paris, concerned about the implications of a trade treaty being negotiated between Britain and France. Later, he travelled on to Pau, Basses Pyrénées, where the family spent Christmas in the Villa des Cèdres.

It is probable that during this period he commissioned the fashionable and successful architect, Auguste Tronquois, to prepare the designs for the new house; most accounts suggest that the design work commenced as early as 1869, but the source for this information has not been found. The reasons why Corbett chose to build are probably related to his political aspirations, the need for a larger family house and, possibly as his personal legacy. He was elected to the Droitwich seat in 1874 and remained as MP until 1892.

THE ARCHITECTS

Why did Corbett choose a French architect and a French style for building? It seems unlikely that it was because his wife was French; she was Irish/British. Nor does it seem likely that he built to assuage any homesickness; she had lived in Worcestershire, and Wales, for more than 15 years before building began. His correspondence offers no answer, but it is clear that Corbett spent much time in France – Paris and Pau - and was fluent in the language.[5] It can be assumed that he was a Francophile.

Auguste Tronquois was born in Seignelay (Yonne) in 1829, the son of a baker. He matriculated at the Ecole des Beaux-Arts on 26 November 1852. He was a pupil of Léon Chaboüillé and then Émile Vaudremer. Tronquois was well known by the later 1860s, not so much for his 1867 publication *Bâtiments pittoresques*,[6] which featured rural estate buildings, as for town houses and apartments in the smart inner suburbs of Paris. According to the Archives Nationales, he was practising as an architect, based originally in the 1st arrondissement of Paris, later in the 8th arrondissement, and at Versailles. He was responsible for numerous private buildings: apartment blocks ('maisons de rapport'), mansions, industrial properties and the Au Gagne Petit Store, 1878 [Fig 4.3], in which year he was made Chevalier de la Légion d'Honneur. Corbett's hotel in Rue de la Paix would have provided him with ample opportunity to become familiar with Tronquois' work.

There can be no doubt that Tronquois provided the designs and specifications for Impney [Figs 4.4, 4.5], and he appears to have been responsible for the execution of the works there until the end of 1874. The drawings were in London by May 1872, for display at the South Kensington International Exhibition of that year. *The Architect* carried the following report:

Fig 4.3. | Au Gagne Petit Store, Avenue de l'Opéra, Paris. Auguste Tronquois, architect, 1878

> We discovered with regret that some drawings are absent from the gallery, having arrived too late, which are also excellent examples of French work, not only in drawing but design. These are four perspectives of a mansion being erected in Warwickshire [*sic*], from the designs M. Tronquois, a well-known Parisian architect. They are hung in the office of the Commissioner for the French Court, M. Sommerard, who will kindly allow any visitor to examine them. The interior views, especially of the staircase and dining-room, are lessons for our English architects, in style and quality of drawing. They are M. Tronquois' own hand-work, and show how valuable are such drawings to a client who can thus see the veritable and ultimate effect before him of the building on which he is about to expend money.[7]

By June that year advertisements were placed seeking tenders 'for erection of carcase for mansion'; the notice referred to drawings, specifications, and quantities prepared by Tronquois, Paris, but the tender was to be sent to Messrs. Arding and Bond, surveyors, of Bedford Row, London.[8] The tenders had to be submitted before 3 o'clock precisely on 27 June. The foundation stone, however, was not laid, by Mr and Mrs Corbett, until Monday, 26 January 1874; Tronquois was present.[9] Why the delay of eighteen months? Gaps in the correspondence

Fig 4.4. | Château Impney, entrance front. [By courtesy of Rod Spollon]

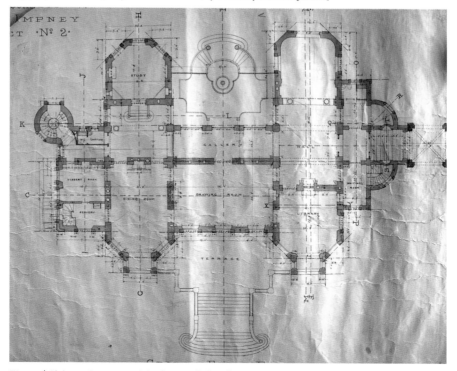

Fig 4.5. | Château Impney, original ground plan. [By courtesy of Rod Spollon]

prevent the full story from being written. However, it appears that the tender process was abandoned. One key factor, inevitably, was cost. In April and May 1873 there was an exchange between Corbett and his surveyors, Arding and Bond. Corbett had thought that he was to allow £12–13,000 for the erection of the carcase but a sum of £20–30,000 was being discussed. The exasperated client wrote that 'I saw the drawings only for a few minutes in Paris, and I believe I never knew the size of the rooms until after Monsr Tronquois had sent the case to you, and he never mentioned to me that the cost would exceed my limit. I never knew of any enlargement.' He was clearly annoyed with his surveyors for, as he saw it, allowing matters to get out of hand in terms of costs but also for their charges. He twice offered to refer the matter to arbitration and by June 1873 he had sought the advice of another architect, T.E. Knightley, on the issues, including the percentage – 2½% – for Arding and Bond, a sum which Corbett considered to be 'monstrous'. He mentioned the possibility of letting a jury decide. In one letter to his solicitor, he asked that questions be put to counsel concerning Tronquois' responsibilities, paying the surveyors' fees and the possibility of being sued by the architect. Arding and Bond were dismissed but their 'large claim' was paid. In the summer of 1873, there were direct negotiations between Corbett and the contractors, Messrs. Wood and Son of Worcester; the client was considering engaging the firm 'without inviting any other tender'. On 4 July Corbett wrote that he would make up his mind 'in a day or two'.

Even after work had commenced, the anxious client continued to fret. A letter dated 6 July 1874, makes reference to a contract price of £17,000 that had been agreed in the preceding month; it was for the 'carcase of the house' and 'with the proviso that the Building was to be 1/7th less than the original plans'. Mr Ridett (L.C. Ridett, an architect who supplied quantities) had been consulted and reported that the contractor's calculations now indicated a 50% increase. The letter ends 'I need not tell you that this House is to me a most troublesome affair.' By November that year he had agreed to an increase to a maximum of £21,000

> provided it includes the Stone Work (not to be cement) leading to the Vestibule, & also the original plan of Stone Work in the Tower; and further that the building be measured up at the finishing of the Carcase, & should it contain less in the quantity of any Material or Materials than contained in Mr Riddett's estimate of Quantities and such amount of value to be deducted for the said sum of £21,000.

In the succeeding paragraph the contractors were advised as follows: 'I have written to Mr Spiers by this post. Monsr Tronquois leaves Paris next Tuesday unless I write or Telegraph him to the contrary.' This appears to signal the handover in terms of responsibility for the execution of the works.

Richard Phené Spiers (1838–1916), was born in Oxford, the eldest son of Richard James Spiers, a hairdresser who became a stationer, bookseller and owner of a china and glass warehouse in the High Street. He was an alderman and later became mayor. Richard, the son, was educated at King's College School and in the engineering department of King's College, London.[10] From 1858 to 1861 he was, unusually for an Englishman, a student at the Ecole des Beaux-Arts in Paris. He became assistant to Matthew Digby Wyatt, then after winning medals and prizes at the RA he travelled abroad with friends for 18 months in 1863, sketching and painting watercolours. He was appointed 'Master in the Class of Architecture' at the Royal Academy in 1870.

As Gavin Stamp has written, 'Spiers's executed works are not numerous', but there is one at Impney. Fourteen drawings, comprising all four elevations, all floor plans, except the basement, and five sheets of sections, survive and are still at Impney; some are annotated 'Mr Wood's copy' or 'Clerk of works copy to be returned to R Phené Spiers at close of job'.[11] All annotations are in English and measurements are in Imperial. The names 'Tronquois and R Phene Spiers Architects' appear at the bottom right-hand corner of many of the drawings. The dates that the clerk received his copies span three years, but the majority are dated 18 December 1874 or 18 January 1875. These can be taken as copies produced in, and issued by, Spiers's office when he took over supervision of the contract for the completion of the building.

Spiers had a drawing exhibited at the Royal Academy in 1877.[12] It was listed in the catalogue as 'Mansion at Impney, near Droitwich, A. Tronquois and R Phené Spiers'. The *Building News* described it as 'a clever colour drawing of exterior in brick, with circular turret and high roof, in a pleasing chateau style of Renaissance, thoroughly French, in feeling and detail'. It is not possible to tell whether the entry was one of the 'original' drawings or a new rendering by Spiers, but it would appear to have been the latter, possibly as one of his attractive watercolours. In the following year, at the 1878 Paris Exhibition, he entered an image of the principal façade – possibly the same image as that which was exhibited at the RA – but the catalogue entry reads 'M. A. Tronquois, architecte'. In the same year the influential French journal, *Le Moniteur des architectes*, published four engravings entitled 'Château à la Campagne', or just 'Château', citing Tronquois, alone, as the architect [Fig 4.6].[13]

The documentary evidence is clear enough that the original design of Impney was solely the work of Tronquois. However Spiers, besides his intermediary role from at least 1874, went on to design the stables. He exhibited a further watercolour of the stabling at the RA in 1877 [Fig 4.7]. It was described as 'in another style, with inclosed yard, but we do not like the brick patterns studded over walls'.

The clerk of works at Impney was also an architect. This was Harrison Fagg, born in 1848 at West Malling, Kent. By 1879 Fagg presented himself as architect, and clerk to Corbett; he had a house in the parish, Dodderhill Villa. He designed some shops, including a coffee tavern (1880), in the High Street, Droitwich, in the timber-framed style of architecture and prepared the specification for alterations to and the repair of the school at Stoke Prior (Wood was the contractor). He went on to become architect for the brewers B. C. Bushell Watkins & Co, of Westerham, Kent.

Fig 4.6. | Château Impney, perspective by Tronquois, published in *Le Moniteur des architectes*, 1878

Fig 4.7. | The stable block at Impney. Watercolour by R. Phené Spiers exhibited at the Royal Academy, 1877. [Victoria & Albert Museum, Prints and Drawings, E.2433]

In June and July 1874, advertisements were placed for banker hands, masons for Bath stone and bricklayers.[14] In May 1875, there were calls for carpenters for 'heavy roofing', and again, in September, when more bricklayers were also needed for the roof and the chimneys.[15] The garden elevation of the house, faced in Fareham brick with Bath stone dressings, bears the date 1875, indicating the date of completion of the carcase. Two years later there was a call for plasterers for the interior.

The *Building News* reported in August 1881 that the hall was having its internal decoration completed by J. Taylor, of Five Ways, Birmingham.[16] The vestibule was painted in buff, green and salmon with gold highlights. The corridor walls were Pompeian red, over a green dado. In Corbett's study the ceiling had a dark fret pattern on a silver ground and the enriched moulded cove had central shields portraying the Arts and Sciences; the wall below was painted in imitation of tapestry in a reddish tone. The staircase and ceiling are of oak and the walls were a full-toned sap-green [Fig 4.8]. The glass was made in 1879 by James Powell & Sons, of Whitefriars, London, with figures of Chaucer, Shakespeare and Spenser, designed by Harry Burrow. The ceiling-mouldings of the drawing-room give a large oval in the centre, about 16 ft. by 13ft., treated with an aerial clouded sky, and cherubs, carrying flambeaux and strewing flowers. The angle-panels have gold grounds, with cameo-heads of Beethoven, Bach, Handel, and Mozart.

In the grounds an elaborate parterre and terrace was laid out immediately in front of the house; it was described as 'one of the neatest in England' to have been designed by Robert Marnock.[17] The park consisted of ornamental waters

Fig 4.8. | Hall and staircase at Impney. [By courtesy of Rod Spollon]

Fig 4.9. | Fishing lake at Impney with the house behind. [By courtesy of Rod Spollon]

[Fig 4.9]: three interconnected lakes with weirs, waterfalls, tree-planted islands and cast-iron bridges. A huge, walled kitchen garden with extensive ranges of glasshouses, supplied by Messrs Clark and Hope, of Birmingham at a cost of £3,000 (all demolished), was laid out to the south of the stable block. An eyecatcher (water tower) stood on the hill to the north of mansion.

ALTERATIONS AND ADDITIONS

There were three lodges on the main road: two survive. The South Lodge has French elements: a round turret and high, conical roof. The list description attributes it to Tronquois but it is more likely to be by John Cotton, a Birmingham architect who worked for Corbett at the Raven Hotel in Droitwich and who designed the North Lodge (1882) at Impney. Cotton's Ravencrest (1891) in the grounds has similar details including a turret.

Electric lighting was introduced in 1886 with a water turbine supplied by Messrs Nicholson and Jennings, of the Old Kent Road, London; the turbine house was on the River Salwarpe.[18] A large, heated glasshouse, known as the fernery, was erected (1890; demolished) in a disused gravel pit that had been transformed into a dell garden; it lay to the east of the entrance portico at about 100 feet from the house.[19] The statistics are interesting: it was 150 feet long by 60 feet wide; 200 tons of rocks were brought from Matlock Bath; there was an artificial stream and pond and electric lighting electricity; and there was an underground passage to the mansion. A fire engine house was built in 1895 to house a Merryweather 'Greenwich'-pattern engine.

Corbett died at Impney on 22 April 1901, at the age of 83; he didn't live long enough to see the publication of an illustrated six-page article in the 'Gardens Old & New' feature in *Country Life*.[20] He had spent the last sixteen and a half years of his life legally separated from his wife. The terms of the settlement included a clause that banned Anna Eliza from coming within 40 miles of Impney and the Welsh estate and no further provision was made for her in his will. Impney passed to his brother, Dr Thomas Corbett, who occupied it for a short time before selling the contents (1906) and leasing the house to a Colonel Spencer who was succeeded by H. Mitchell, a Birmingham pen manufacturer. In 1925 the site was bought by James Ward, who had helped to build the original mansion.[21] It was converted into a hotel, one of the guests being P. G. Wodehouse who, according to the *Sunday Times* for 27 March 1938, 'wrote some of his delectable books' while staying at Impney. It may have been the model for Sir Buckstone Abbot's Walsingford Hall, otherwise Abbot's Folly, one of the least attractive stately homes in the country, in Wodehouse's *Summer Moonshine* (1938). It was first named Château Impney in 1949. Internal alterations were undertaken in the 1920s and after the War but the most damaging works – the removal of the *porte cochère* and the construction of the ugly new entrance and north extensions – were not carried out until 1970–2. Impney closed as a hotel during the Covid-19 pandemic.

NOTES

1. Nikolaus Pevsner, *The Buildings of England: Worcestershire*, 1968, p.9.
2. S. E. Fryer, revised by Anita McConnell, 'Corbett, John', in *Oxford Dictionary of National Biography*, September 2004. See also Barbara Middlemass and Joe Hunt, *John Corbett Pillar of Salt 1817–1901*, 1985, and John Richard Hodges, *Chateau Impney*, 2017, and *John Corbett – 1817–1901, The Worcestershire Salt King*, vols 1 & 2, 2010.
3. *Worcester Journal*, 15 June 1872.
4. Lyn Blewett, 'From Manor to Mansion: the Ownership of Impney', in Derek Hurst *et al.*, *Dodderhill Through the Ages*, 2011, pp.153–6.
5. Copies of ten of Corbett's letters are in the possession of Rod Spollon, Château Impney. The whereabouts of the originals is not known.
6. Auguste Tronquois, *Bâtiments pittoresques: recueil de cottages, villas, châlets, bâtiments de communs et de basse-cour ... exécutés dans les environs de Paris*, 1867.
7. *The Architect*, 18 May 1872, p.254.
8. *Worcester Journal*, 15 June 1872, and *Building News*, 21 June 1872, p.513.
9. *Bromsgrove and Droitwich Messenger*, 31 January 1874.

10. A. T. Bolton, revised by Gavin Stamp, 'Spiers, Richard Phené', in *Oxford Dictionary of National Biography*, 2004.
11. The drawings and Corbett's album of photographs are in the possession of Rod Spollon, Château Impney. The author is grateful for Mr Spollon's permission to reproduce copies of the material.
12. 'Architecture at the Royal Academy', *Building News*, 4 May 1877, p.452, 18 May 1877, p.486.
13. *Le Moniteur des architectes*, vol.12, 1878, pp.48, 79, 80, 128, 157 & 158 and plates 15, 21, 37–38 & 49.
14. *Worcestershire Chronicle*, 20 & 30 June and 26 September 1874.
15. *Worcestershire Chronicle*, 8 May & 18 September 1875, and *Gloucester Journal*, 24 July 1875.
16. *Building News*, vol.41, 1881, p.183, and *Birmingham Daily Post*, 3 August 1881.
17. *Gardeners' Chronicle*, 1 October 1881, p.427.
18. *Worcestershire Chronicle*, 14 August 1886.
19. *Journal of Horticulture and Cottage Gardener*, vol.28, 1894, pp.53–4.
20. *Country Life*, 11 May 1901, pp.592–8.
21. *Gloucestershire Echo*, 13 June 1925.

5 · 'Too French': the impact of Dusillion's Hope house on Victorian architecture

JOSEPH SPECKLIN

THE RISE AND FALL OF THE HOPE HOUSE

The project for this house can be traced back to 14 June 1847, when the French architect Pierre-Charles Dusillion was introduced to the members of the Royal Institute of British Architects. George Godwin or one of his collaborators noted in *The Builder*: 'We hear, and we confess, with some surprise, that M. Dusillon [sic] has been brought over by Mr. H. T. Hope to build his new house at the corner of Down-street, in Piccadilly. Mr. Donaldson is to be associated with him in carrying it out'.[1]

Henry Thomas Hope (1807–62), from a family of Dutch bankers of Scottish descent, was a wealthy businessman and Conservative MP. He inherited two magnificent houses from his father, Thomas Hope, a famous patron of the arts known for his contribution to the Regency style: these two buildings were the country house of Deepdene, near Dorking, in Surrey, and a London town house in Duchess Street, which housed his famous art collection. Henry Thomas Hope kept and reshaped Deepdene, but he decided to give up the house of Duchess Street and to build a new mansion in a more fashionable neighbourhood of the West End, between Mayfair and the Green Park [Fig 5.2].

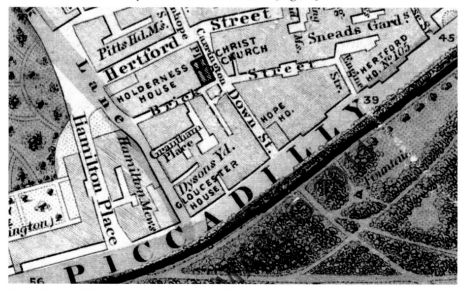

Fig 5.2. | Detail of Stanford's *Map of London* (1872), showing the context for Hope house.

Fig 5.1. | 'Mansion of H. T. Hope, Esq., M.P., Piccadilly, London. – Messrs. Dusillion and Donaldson, architects', from George Godwin, *Buildings & Monuments*, 1850.

the Hope house with new elements characteristic of Victorian architecture, like the three-storey bow windows. The shape of these bow windows influenced the aspect of the front of other nearby buildings, still visible today in Down Street.

In due course the Junior Athenaeum ran into financial difficulties, and decided to dissolve at the end of 1931. The disused clubhouse was destroyed in July 1935 and replaced two years later by the Athenaeum Court, an eleven-storey concrete building designed by George Mountford Adie of the Adie, Button and Partners architectural firm, which had already built the nearby Park Lane Hotel.[13] This building was altered in the 1970s and again in the 1990s, and today houses the Athenaeum Hotel.[14]

AN ANGLO-FRENCH DESIGN

Hope's mansion was billed as a collaborative work between a British architect, Thomas Leverton Donaldson, and a French one, Pierre-Charles Dusillion. A newspaper article of 1868 implied that Dusillion was mostly employed for the interior decoration.[15] In fact, his artistic contribution is obvious throughout the whole composition, not least the front. Henry-Russell Hitchcock considered that the house had been designed by Dusillion and erected under the supervision of Donaldson, who probably did not significantly modify the plans of his colleague, or only in a few details such as the original Belgravia-style portico.[16]

Born in Paris in 1804, Dusillion was the son of a draughtsman who was a collaborator of Antoine Vaudoyer, architect of the Institut de France. Thanks to Vaudoyer's endorsement, he was admitted and trained in the Ecole des Beaux-Arts. During the 1820s he worked as an assistant architect on some of the great neoclassical building projects in the French capital. He was also an assistant to a Swiss architect settled in Paris, Joseph-Antoine Froelicher, who worked mainly for the French aristocracy of the Faubourg Saint-Germain. Froelicher was a career model for Dusillion, who is mostly known for the Parisian buildings and the country houses that he restored or built between the late 1830s and the 1870s. Amongst his well-known works are Schloss Schadau, on the banks of Lake Thun (Switzerland), and the restoration and completion of one of the most famous châteaux of the Loire Valley, Azay-le-Rideau.[17]

In 1835, a few years after he established himself as an independent architect, Dusillion designed, for a contractor named Genaille, a house which can be considered as a manifesto for the Renaissance Revival. It still stands, well restored, in the Rue Vaneau (7th arrondissement). Fifteen years after its construction, some of its features were to recur in the Hope house: a prominent mansard roof and a rich ornamentation, including delicate bas-reliefs and coloured marble plaques [Fig 5.6].

On either side of a pediment carrying a portrait of Renaissance architect Philibert Delorme, the cornice of the piano nobile on the Genaille house bears an inscription in Latin: *Bona aedificatio tres habet conditiones. Commoditatem, firmitatem et delectationem* ('Wel building hath three Conditions, Commodity,

Fig 5.6. | House by Dusillion in Rue de Vaneau, Paris, for the builder P.-J.-F. Genaille, 1835. [Author]

Firmnesse, and Delight'). This motto is a derivative from Vitruvius' principles on 'firmitas, utilitas, venustas' (solidity, utility and pleasantness), as restated in the translation from Latin in Henry Wotton's *Elements of Architecture*, first published in 1624. Thus, Dusillion's knowledge about Vitruvian theory seems to arise from an English author of the Jacobean era.

The Renaissance Revival manifesto in Rue Vaneau constituted a second decisive stage in the development of this historicist style, a decade after the construction, by J.-M.-D. Biet, of the famous 'François Premier House' in the same district of Paris. Dusillion indeed went much further than Biet, who had simply attached to a neoclassical building the decorative elements of an authentic sixteenth-century house, the Hôtel de Chabouillé, dismantled at Moret-sur-Loing, near Fontainebleau, and returned there in 1955.[18] It should be noted that an obscure biographical compilation published in 1861 contains a suspiciously long note on Dusillion – too flattering to be accidental – which claims the François Premier House as one of the early works of the young architect.[19]

The house in Rue Vaneau featured in several periodicals of its time. It is Dusillion's tribute to both the classical tradition and the French Renaissance styles of the Valois era. It exerted an indisputable influence on Parisian architecture and foreshadows the main characteristics of the Hope house.

Apart from Hope's house, Dusillion is not known for any other buildings in the UK, but he is mentioned among the foreign architects who presented a project for the Crystal Palace.[20]

For a foreign architect who wanted to build on the British side of the Channel, it was almost a necessity to work in partnership with a well-established British architect. For this role, Thomas Leverton Donaldson was the right man in the right place.

As a result of his Grand Tour, after the Napoleonic wars and his training at the Royal Academy, Donaldson established many close contacts with young continental architects. He referred to French architects like Hittorff, Nepveu and Blouet as his friends.[21] Due to these connections, he was nominated secretary for foreign correspondence of the RIBA. Donaldson was very open-minded to innovations and to the use of French materials. For instance, in 1847, he visited the quarries of Caen, Normandy, with Charles Harriot Smith to select the best varieties of stone for the Hope mansion.[22] Though this stone was easy to work, it was quite vulnerable to the London atmosphere, so Donaldson took Smith's advice and decided to protect the house's mouldings and cornices by covering them with thin sheets of lead.[23]

Less famous in the field of arts than his father, Thomas Hope, or than his brother, Alexander Beresford Hope, who was an influential promoter of the Gothic Revival, Henry Hope was also considered as a connoisseur and a man of taste. A member of many learned societies such as the Dilettanti, he edited and wrote a preface to his father's *Historical Essay on Architecture* in 1840.

Hope lived with a French woman, Anne Adèle Bichat, whom he married in 1851. Their only daughter Henrietta was his heir and married well, later becoming Countess Lincoln and then Duchess of Newcastle. Hope may have believed he was himself of French descent. Indeed, *Burke's Landed Gentry* claims that the Scottish ancestors of the Hopes came from France in 1537 with the retinue of Madeleine de Valois, wife of James V of Scotland.[24]

Despite his artistic culture and his personal links with France, Hope's interest in French architecture was recent when he hired Dusillion. Indeed, in the 1830s, when he recast the family's country house at Deepdene, he commissioned from the architects Alexander Roos and Thomas Liddell a classical building similar to an Italian palazzo [Fig 5.7].

Before Dusillion's encroachment on the London architectural scene, Frenchmen were already ubiquitous in the field of English decorative arts. Some high-class French craftsmen worked on the Hope house, including the stained-glass workshop of Laurent, Gsell et Compagnie (as this firm was known at that date) and the cast-iron manufactory of Val d'Osne, directed by Jean-Pierre-Victor André. The latter produced the iron railing, which was admired by many Englishmen, especially George Godwin, and which proudly bore Hope's monogram [Fig 5.8].

Because the ironwork of Hope's mansion was so well received, the employment of French craftsmen was even discussed for the railings of the British Museum. But this proposal was disputed in October 1850 by the *Civil Engineer and Architect's Journal*: 'Let the trustees of the Museum offer even two thirds of

Fig 5.7. | Deepdene House, Surrey, in 1842, as remodelled for H. T. Hope by Alexander Roos, from Brayley's *Topographical History of Surrey*, vol. V, 1850.

Fig 5.8. | Iron railing designed by J.-P.-V. André for the Hope house, Piccadilly, from George Godwin, *Buildings & Monuments*, 1850.

the price that was given by Mr Hope, and they will find plenty of English manufacturers who will produce railings quite equal to the fancy-price foreign article
in Piccadilly.'[25] The museum railings were eventually cast by John Walker of York.

A MIXED RECEPTION

Between 1848 and 1851, when Londoners discovered the new mansion built on
Piccadilly for the wealthy Henry Thomas Hope, it met with widespread admiration. Besides the *Builder* article already cited, it was mentioned in a guidebook
published by John Weale and, later, the 1855 edition of John Timbs' *Curiosities of
London*.[26] However, harsh criticisms were also expressed by other authors, with
comments mixing disgust and mockery. As reported by Frederick Locker-Lampson, the great Charles Dickens himself stated that the Hope house 'looked as if
it had had its face scratched and then covered with strips of sticking-plaster'.[27]

Some features of the house were misunderstood or despised by some critics
but praised by the connoisseurs. For example, in the 1849 *British Almanac*, an
author wrote about the twin windows: 'The windows, consisting of two openings
put together beneath an entablature and heavy segmental pediment, are most
amorphous compositions'.[28] However, two years later, in a lecture at the Royal
Academy, C. R. Cockerell stated: 'In England … the window is the great characteristic; and so in the north of France, under Phil[ibert] de l'Orme, they grew into the
most important features, and might be called the Fenestral order, the binated windows used in Mr. Hope's new house, Piccadilly, were commendable in this respect,
and conveyed the idea of abundant light and large admission of sun's rays.'[29]

In 1848 the *Civil Engineer and Architect's Journal* made a disobliging comparison between Bridgewater House, recently built by Charles Barry on the eastern
edge of Green Park, and its contemporary, H. T. Hope's house, on the northern
edge of the same park. 'The latter', wrote the journalist, 'is such a vile compound
of uncouthness and deformity, as to be nothing less than marvellous. That pre-
cious sample of design is said to be by some foreign architect, – which is the only
thing to console us.'[30]

Beyond the obvious nationalism of its last sentence, this critic pointed to the
shocking contrast between two architectural styles, the well-established Ital-
ianate or 'Italian *palazzo* style', inspired by the Italian Renaissance and mastered
by Barry, and a new 'French' style inspired by the Renaissance Revival experiments conducted across the Channel by lesser-known architects like Dusillion.

Bridgewater House already borrowed from Renaissance Revival features, like
the ringed columns of its porch, but it was also the swan song of a stricter classicism, as indicated by its rooftop hidden by the balustrade [Fig 5.9].[31]

The nationalist overtone of some critics can be linked to the quest for a true
national style. In 1856 an article in *The Globe* took a position against Benjamin
Hall's proposition to open the competition for the new Government offices to
continental architects:

We differ *toto caelo* from an ingenious correspondent of the *Times*, who thinks that Sir Benjamin Hall's proposal to admit the competition of continental architects would facilitate a harmonious variety of styles. We do not think Mr. Hope's House, for example, produces by any means a harmonious variety in Piccadilly. It is too French in its whole design and decoration for the site where it stands. A practised eye ought to be able to decide from the view of a building – 'That building must be in London – or Paris'.[32]

Yet despite such criticisms of the French Renaissance style, that tradition of architecture was almost as suitable as the medieval Gothic to Romantic tastes, and had already been studied and admired by some Victorian architects and art theorists. At the dawn of the Victorian era, French Renaissance buildings had already been elevated to the rank of role model by Pugin in his *Contrasts*, in which an elaborate and picturesque façade in the Rue du Gros-Horloge, Rouen, was opposed to the cold classicism of John Soane's house [Fig 5.10].[33]

Nationalism aside, the sheer conservatism of many critics weighed against a warm reception for the house. In 1849, the *Civil Engineer and Architect's Journal*, which nicknamed Hope's house 'hopeful mansion', blamed the deformities

Fig 5.9. | Bridgewater House, St James, London, garden front. Sir Charles Barry, architect, 1845–8.

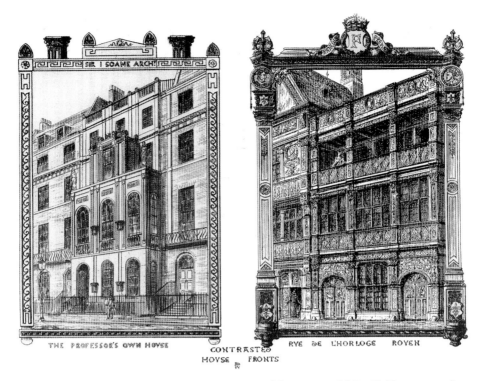

Fig 5.10. | 'The Professor's own house', i.e. Sir John Soane's house, Lincoln's Inn Fields, contrasted with an early Renaissance house in Rue du Gros-Horloge, Rouen. Drawings by the younger Pugin from the first edition of *Contrasts*, 1836. The Rouen front, perhaps drawn as early as 1824, was the only foreign example in *Contrasts*.

caused by too much innovation: 'Rash and fool-hardy innovation is, of course, to be discountenanced; and such unlucky and prodigiously queer originality as we got in the new Coal Exchange, and in the new hopeful mansion in Piccadilly, is to be deprecated most earnestly.'[34]

Many of the criticisms of the Hope house took aim at the novelty of its architectural style, which relied more on the profusion of its colourful decoration than on the purity of its general lines. Dickens's criticism, mentioned above, alluded to 'the introduction of flat slabs of polished red granite between the windows ... a novelty in domestic architecture'.[35] Such decorative processes, widespread in Parisian architecture, were already in use in London, but mainly on shop-fronts or in the interior architecture of drinking establishments.

A good example of a profusely decorated Renaissance Revival shopfront was published in 1846 in the *Illustrated London News*: Piver's perfumery in Regent Street, designed 'by a distinguished French architect'.[36] This latter is unnamed in the article but the shop seems quite close stylistically to Dusillion's known works, like the Café de la Banque near the Place des Victoires in Paris.

A satirical article in *The Atlas* mocked the apparent similarity between a fancy patrician house like the Hope house and a flashy gin-palace: 'At No. 116, Piccadilly, on the site of some ancient beershop, has arisen within the past year a large house, looking exactly like an exaggerated gin-palace. Whether the stones still retained a taste of the old occupants of the place, or whether the reason is to be found in the native barbarism of the persons concerned, we know not; but Modern architecture has rarely been disgraced by such a tawdry-staring specimen as the mansion in question.' Taking its cue from the vandalism committed on the front door by an anonymous offender, the article continued, tongue in cheek: 'It may be, after all, that some drunken fellow, late at night, mistaking the erection for a gin-shop, wrenched off the knocker in the vain attempt to gain admittance.'[37]

This humorous article hints that this kind of architecture, though apparently luxurious, was in fact addressed to the poor taste of the uneducated masses. We can already find a similar point of view, twenty years earlier, in an 1833 illustration by George Cruikshank, depicting a ragged crowd of drunkards leaving a luxurious so-called 'gin-temple'.[38]

INFLUENCE OF THE HOPE HOUSE

Henry-Russell Hitchcock, who rediscovered Dusillion's work in the 1950s, argues that the Hope house is one of the few early examples, alongside Wrest Park, Bedfordshire, of the French taste in English architecture.[39]

Fifteen or twenty years after its completion, the silhouette of the house was not so unusual in the metropolitan landscape. Many buildings of the 1860s by British architects took up the same features, like the mansard roof. They were gradually integrated into the Victorian style, whose eclecticism reflects the balance between the quest for a national identity and an expression of the cosmopolitanism of the largest global empire.

For example, James Stevens Curl notes that French Renaissance styles were employed by Thomas Cundy III in Grosvenor Place, where quasi-Parisian town houses, complete with tall French roofs, were built in 1868.[40] We can also mention Brook House, Park Lane (1867–9), by Thomas Henry Wyatt. These examples show a convergence between the Victorian historicist style and the French Second Empire style, which had already been foreshadowed in the late 1830s and the early 1840s, when Dusillion and others revived Renaissance motifs in the Parisian landscape of the July Monarchy.

The influence of the Hope house on London and British architecture may have gone even beyond the Victorian era, if we believe David Watkin when he refers to this building as 'in a fussy proto-Edwardian style'.[41] 'Proto-Edwardian' or 'Second Empire "avant la lettre"', as suggested by Hitchcock,[42] the house was indeed a pioneering work of art and a good example of the conflicting but enriching exchanges that have always taken place across the breadth of the Channel.

1. *The Builder*, 19 June 1847, p.287. This information was then spread by several newspapers under the title 'Importation of Foreign Architects to Build British Houses' (*Daily Advertiser*, 22 June 1847; *Home News*, 24 June 1847).

2. 'From £12 to £120.000!': *Middlesex Advertiser*, 22 May 1936.

3. *Morning Post*, 24 November 1847.

4. *The Builder*, 20 October 1849, p.493. Also published in George Godwin, *Buildings & Monuments, Modern and Mediaeval*, 1850, pp.60–2.

5. '*The Builder*, 1 December 1849, p.572.

6. *Punch*, vol.17, July–December 1849, p.257.

7. Arthur Irwin Dasent, *Piccadilly in Three Centuries,* 1920 edn, p.145; Ralph Nevill, *Romantic London*, [1928], p.77.

8. Henry B. Wheatley, *Round About Piccadilly and Pall Mall*, 1870, p.209.

9. *Saunders's News-Letter*, 16 May 1868.

10. *The Builder*, 30 October 1875, p.966.

11. *The Standard*, 20 November 1868.

12. *The Builder*, 24 March 1888, p.212.

13. Harold P. Clunn, *The Face of London*, 1937 edn, p.496.

14. Andrew Jones, *The Buildings of Green Park*, 2020, pp.88–9.

15. *The Standard*, 20 November 1868.

16. Henry-Russell Hitchcock, 'Second Empire avant la lettre', *Gazette des Beaux-Arts*, vol.XLII, 1953, pp.115–44.

17. Joseph Specklin, 'Pierre-Charles Dusillion et l'architecture néorenaissance', *Livraisons d'histoire de l'architecture*, nr.23, 2012|1, pp.87–105.

18. Marie-Agnès Arhan, 'Le Quartier François Iᵉʳ', in Dominique Leborgne (ed.), *Les Champs-Elysées et leur quartier*, 1988, p.120.

19. Victor Lacaine, *Biographies et nécrologies des hommes marquants du XIXᵉ siècle*, vol.XII, 1861, p.167.

20. William Cubitt, 'Report of the Building Committee on the Plans Submitted', *The Sun*, 3 June 1850.

21. Thomas L. Donaldson, 'Memoir of Monsieur Charles Frederick Nepveu, Architect, of Versailles', *Papers Read at the Royal Institute of British Architects* (session 1862-63), 1863, p.11.

22. Wyatt Papworth, 'The Late Professor Donaldson: His Connection with the Institute', *Transactions of the RIBA*, new series, vol.II, 1886, p.100. For C. H. Smith and Caen stone, see Edward John Gillin, 'Stones of Science: Charles Harriot Smith and the Importance of Geology in Architecture, 1834–64', *Architectural History*, vol.59, 2016, pp.281–310.

23. *Journal of the Society of the Arts*, 2 March 1860, p.249; Shirley Forster Murphy (ed.), *Our Homes, and How to Make them Healthy*, 1883, p.269.

24. John Burke, *A Genealogical and Heraldic Dictionary of the Landed Gentry* (small paper edition), vol.IV, 1838, p.458.

25. *Civil Engineer and Architect's Journal*, October 1850, p.336.

26. John Weale, *London Exhibited in 1851*, [1851], p.730; John Timbs, *Curiosities of London,*1855, pp.488–9.

27. Frederick Locker-Lampson, *My Confidences: An Autobiographical Sketch Addressed to My Descendants*, 1896, p. 19. Locker-Lampson mistakenly sets this anecdote in 1843–4. In all likelihood he was confused with a later encounter with the famous novelist, in 1848 or shortly after.

28. *British Almanac of the Society for the Diffusion of Useful Knowledge, for the Year of Our Lord 1849*, 1848, p.244.

29. 'Professor Cockerell's Lectures on Architecture, at the Royal Academy', *The Builder*, 26 January 1850, p.38.

30. *Civil Engineer and Architect's Journal*, October 1848, p. 321.

31. Rosemary Hill also considered that Bridgewater House, as 'one of the last great private mansions to be built in the capital, belonged already, as a building type, to an earlier era': 'Introduction: Architecture and the 1840s', in Rosemary Hill and Michael Hall (eds), *The 1840s, Studies in Victorian Architecture and Design*, vol.I, 2008, p.14).

32. *The Globe*, 31 May 1856.

33. 'Contrasted House Fronts', in A. Welby

Pugin, *Contrasts; Or, A Parallel Between the Noble Edifices of the Fourteenth and Fifteenth Centuries, and Similar Buildings of the Present Days,* 1836.

34. *Civil Engineer and Architect's Journal,* March 1849, p.67.

35. Locker-Lampson, p.319.

36. *Illustrated London News,* 22 August 1846, p.128. According to this article, the shopfront was built 'in the richly decorated style of the age of Louis XIV [sic] under the superintendence of M. Cambon, the celebrated Parisian decorator'. The contractors were Winsland and Holland.

37. *The Atlas,* 8 December 1849.

38. 'Gin-temple Turn-out at Church-time', in George Cruikshank and John Wight, *Sunday in London,* 1833. See also 'Gin Palaces and the Transformation of the Urban Public House', in James Steven Curl, *Victorian Architecture. Diversity & Invention,* 2007, pp.533–44.

39. Hitchcock, p.141.

40. Curl, pp.427–8.

41. David Watkin, *'Thomas Hope's house in Duchess Street', Apollo,* vol.159, no.505, March 2004, pp.31–9.

42. Hitchcock, *op. cit.*

6 · Two French Monasteries in England

PETER HOWELL

Anticlericalism grew in France during the Third Republic. In 1901 the Law of Associations suppressed nearly all religious houses and confiscated their property. It was followed in 1905 by the separation of Church and State. But this was the end of a long story which went back to the Second Empire.

The Carthusian Order, which had been founded in the twelfth century, was governed from the Grande Chartreuse, near Grenoble. In 1863 Bishop Clifford of Clifton visited the Grande Chartreuse, where the Prior talked of his anxiety about the hostile attitude of the French Government to the religious orders. The Bishop suggested the site of the medieval Carthusian house at Witham in Somerset for an English foundation, but it turned out to be unsuitable. However, the two commissaries sent to see the property met Bishop Grant of Southwark, who invited them to make a foundation in his diocese. A French priest, the Abbé Denis, was sent by Grant to build a church at West Grinstead, in Sussex. He asked the Prior of the Grande Chartreuse to contribute, and the Prior asked the Abbé to look out for a suitable site for a charterhouse in England. Bishop Grant was keen on the proposal, noting that 'my diocese is renowned for its healthy situation and the salubrity of its climate'.[1] Grant died in 1870, but his successor Monsignor Danell was also enthusiastic.

The site found was Parknowle (formerly Picknoll), at Cowfold near Horsham, Sussex. This was for sale freehold with 110 acres.[2] The owner, William Percival Boxall, was a Protestant, and so the three monks sent to negotiate met him in secular clothes. Two monks and an Irish brother were sent to conclude the purchase. Boxall moved out in February 1873. When he found out who they were, he was friendly. The name was changed to Parkminster, though the official title is St Hugh's Charterhouse, after St Hugh of Lincoln, who was Prior of the Witham house before becoming Bishop of Lincoln in 1186. In the same year the monks bought more land to ensure their solitude. The estate eventually amounted to 622 acres. In 1874 Bishop Danell ordained a member of the community to the priesthood, the first Carthusian ordained in England since the Reformation. In 1875 the architect Clovis Normand came on a visit, and in 1877 the foundation stone of the new monastery was laid. By 1882 there were five choir monks and eight laybrothers. In the next year the first Prior was appointed, and brought eight monks and three laybrothers from the Grande Chartreuse. The building was completed in 1883, and the church was consecrated.

The architect appointed, Clovis Normand (1830–1909), was born at Hesdin

Fig 6.1. | Quarr Abbey, vaulting over sanctuary. [Edmund Harris]

in Picardy. He had begun as a carpenter, but became a pupil of the diocesan architect Alexandre Grigny. In his career of forty years he directed 670 chantiers and built 45 churches, renovating many others. Most of his work is in and around Hesdin. He entered the competition for the Sacré Coeur in Paris. His chef d'oeuvre was the church of Notre Dame des Ardents at Arras, vaulted and with an apse and spire, in the 'Romano-Byzantine' style. In 1872–5 he built the Chartreuse de Notre Dame des Prés at Neuville-sous-Montreuil in the Pas de Calais. The Montreuil monks moved to Parkminster in 1901, together with the novices from the houses at Bosserville and Sélignac.

The new monastery was on a huge scale, in a Romanesque style [Fig 6.2]. It is claimed that those disapproving of its extravagance included Cardinal Manning and Queen Victoria. The order was wealthy, because of its Chartreuse liqueur. Six to seven hundred workers used Horsham stone, freestone from Bath, flagstones from Belgium, and 60,000 bricks every fortnight, from kilns on the site. Outside the gatehouse, on its left, is the extern chapel of St Roseline, for local Catholics. It was designed by 'a friend of the order', and built in 1939. It contains three statues by Philip Lindsey Clark. Communion is distributed through an iron grille. There are three cloisters. The first, entered through the gatehouse, has the church in front, with the refectory on the left, and the former Brothers' chapel, now used

Fig 6.2. | St Hugh's Charterhouse, Parkminster, from the air. Clovis Normand, architect, 1877–83. [Jeremy Shapiro]

Fig 6.3. | St Hugh's Charterhouse, church exterior, seen from across the great cloister. [Prior of St Hugh's Charterhouse]

Fig 6.4. | St Hugh's Charterhouse, church interior. [Prior of St Hugh's Charterhouse]

as a library, on the right. On the left of the courtyard is the kitchen and beyond it Boxall's former house of 1866, now the guesthouse. On the right is the Obedience Court, which has the Brothers' cells above the arcades, and on the ground floor the 'obediences', the carpenter's shop, bindery, and beyond these the workshops, forge, laundry, and garages. The printing equipment originally at Montreuil was moved here in 1913, but ceased operation in 1954.

The church is on the main axis [Fig 6.3]. Its spire is 203 feet high. The statue of St Hugh on the gable over the entrance is by Louis Noel of Paris (1839–1925) who executed most of the statuary on the buildings. The apse [Fig 6.4] has a mural in the centre showing the apotheosis of St Hugh, by Antoine Sublet (1821–97), an artist particularly associated with the Carthusians. (There was an exhibition of his work at the Grande Chartreuse in 2022). The original altar survives, and there is a small altar in front of it. Around the walls are stalls, made in Lille. A stone screen with two altars and paintings of St Bruno and St John the Baptist, by Sublet, and a crucifix by Noel, separates the sanctuary and Fathers' choir from the Brothers' choir, originally for the lay brothers, who can now sit in either choir, as they wish. The marquetry floor is of ebony, teak, bird's eye maple, and oak. On the right of the church is a quadrangle surrounded by twelve small chapels, for individual Masses.

Fig 6.5. | St Hugh's Charterhouse, refectory. [Prior of St Hugh's Charterhouse]

On the left is the 'little cloister' which links the church, the refectory and chapter house. Beyond are the Prior's quarters and novitiate. The third, or 'great cloister', is surrounded by the 34 hermitages for the monks. Each little house has a ground floor for the chopping of wood for the stove, and any other manual work, while the upper floor has a bed in an alcove, a prie-dieu, and a desk, all in fine Gothic woodwork. Each has a garden behind. The great cloister is 377 feet wide and 440 feet long. The total length of the three cloisters is a little over a kilometre.

Meals are eaten in the refectory [Fig 6.5] only on Sundays, feast days, and after the death of a monk. Since the Second Vatican Council the laybrothers eat with the monks. At other times meals are served through a hatch at each house. No meat is eaten, but fish three times a week and eggs twice. The vaulted refectory has a stone pulpit for the reader. The large panelled library, off the great cloister, over the chapter house, has a carved wooden roof and galleries with carrels beneath, and contains 50,000 books. The vaulted Fathers' chapter house, on the left of the church, which has wooden panelling and benches, and a stone altar, is decorated with murals by Sublet showing the Crucifixion and the martyrdom of the eighteen London Carthusians [Fig 6.10]. Two were martyred in 1535, and the rest after the house was closed in 1537, apart from one who died in prison in 1540. Three have been canonised, and the rest beatified. (Their martyrdom was similarly represented at other Charterhouses, including those at Naples and El Paular.) Before the Reformation there were nine Carthusian monasteries in England, and St Hugh's was the first and only new foundation since then. Within the great cloister, on the axis of the church, is the cemetery, with a tall crucifix.

In the first edition of *The Buildings of England: Sussex* (1965) Ian Nairn wrote that 'the plan is magnificent ... The outward-facing walls are entirely blank, a reflection of the rigorous, contemplative discipline. Alas, the design does not keep up this standard. Imported bodily from across the Channel, it represents the French Gothic Revival [*sic*] at its weakest and harshest. The impression of being in the outskirts of somewhere like Béthune or Arras is overwhelming'.[3] French nineteenth-century architecture is now more kindly judged.

St Hugh's, which is listed Grade II*, was renovated in 1990 with a 33% grant from English Heritage, the architect being John Warren, of Horsham. Each monk now has his own lavatory, shower and basin. In 2018 there were 24 monks, including 10 brothers, from 17 nationalities.

The style of Romanesque at Parkminster is, as one would expect, typical of Northern France, and distinctly un-English, but it is expertly handled and the whole complex is most impressive.

It is unlikely that Dom Paul Bellot would have admired Parkminster. He certainly did not like the Abbey of Sainte Cécile at Solesmes, founded in 1866 for Benedictine nuns, and in a characteristic French 19th-century Gothic. The Benedictine Order was revived in France in 1833 by Dom Prosper Guéranger. He bought the old Priory of Solesmes, near Le Mans. The foundation, dedicated to St Peter, was raised to the status of abbey by Gregory XVI in 1837. When the Law of Associations was passed in 1901, the Abbot, Dom Paul Delatte, decided that the community should move to England. He probably chose the Isle of Wight because of the house of nuns of Pax Cordis at Ventnor, founded in 1882 from Liège. The Solesmes monks first leased Appuldurcombe House, a fine eighteenth-century mansion now in the care of English Heritage. A temporary church of wood and corrugated iron was built to the design of Dom Jules Mellet, who had designed the large additions at Solesmes not long before.

The lease of Appuldurcombe was due to run out in 1908. Bishop Cahill of Portsmouth recommended Quarr, where there were remains of a medieval Cistercian monastery, founded in 1132. In 1907 the monks bought Quarr Abbey House, a gabled Victorian house where Princess Beatrice and Prince Henry of Battenberg had spent their honeymoon, and where Queen Victoria had watched the Cowes Regatta with Kaiser Wilhelm. The temporary church was moved there.

A member of the community was Dom Paul Bellot. Born in 1876 in Paris, his father was a surveyor. In 1894–1901 he studied at the Ecole des Beaux Arts in Paris, under Marcel Lambert (best known as architect to the château of Versailles). He profited from the instruction in planning (the French speciality), but had to design 'kilometres of cornices, hundreds of porticoes, armies of columns, of capitals, of everything you can imagine in this genre'.[4] As a student, he travelled in Spain. In 1902 he joined Solesmes, and was clothed at Appuldurcombe. Professed in 1904, he was ordained priest in 1911. In 1906 he was sent to design a new monastery at Oosterhout in the Netherlands, for the monks of Wisques. This striking brick complex is sadly no longer the home of a Benedictine community. The next year he was called back to design a new monastery at Quarr [Fig 6.6].

For this task he was assisted by the surveyor Hugh Chidgley (later Mayor of Hackney). Edward Goldie, who designed the church and other buildings for the Benedictine nuns of Solesmes, who had moved to Ryde, acted, when required, as an arbitrator. In ten and a half months the monks' cells, refectory, chapter house, library, and three sides of the cloister were built. The church was begun in 1911, and consecrated the next year. The guest house was added in 1913–14. Most of the Victorian house was retained, but simplified, as was its stable court.

Fig 6.6. | Quarr Abbey, entrance to church and monastery. Dom Paul Bellot, architect, 1911–14. [Edmund Harris]

Quarr Abbey (as the monastery became in 1937) is a masterpiece of brick construction. Bellot had been obliged to use brick at Oosterhout, because of the lack of local stone, and he liked the fact that the colour and patterns made other architectural decoration unnecessary. He spoke of juggling with them, as 'fireworks'. At Quarr almost two million were used. They came from Belgium, and the transport cost more than the bricks. The variety of colour in them was exploited by Bellot – pink, orange, blue-grey and violet. Nikolaus Pevsner, who was bowled over on his visit in the mid-1960s, wrote:

> Paul Bellot was a virtuoso in brick. All is brick and all has to be done angularly; for such is the brick's nature. Instead of pointed arches triangular heads. Stepped gables for the low façade of the church and for the entrance to the abbey, cut-back friezes and stepped patterns of all kinds. They are … curiously reminiscent of Gaudi. Inside the church, and also the chapter house and refectory, Paul Bellot repeats one powerful motif: transverse pointed brick arches carrying the roofs, and that is a Catalan motif as well, used in religious and secular architecture, and especially similar to Quarr in the Cistercian monastery of Poblet. But it is also present in such South French Cistercian buildings as Le Thoronet. But Spain altogether must have impressed Paul Bellot most; for the tremendous arches inside the E tower of the church, dazzling with the arched openings pierced in the spandrels, are inspired in their crossing – two diagonal ribs and four running from the middle of one side to the middle of the next – by the Mosque at Cordova.

The way in which the four immensely high narrow windows in the E wall are cut into by the ribs in the tower and the series of open arches in the spandrels is brilliant indeed and establishes Dom Paul Bellot beyond doubt as one of the pioneers of C20 Expressionism.[5]

Moorish influence can be traced to Bellot's visit to Spain. There is a clear similarity to the work of Hendrik Berlage, with whom Bellot had a slight acquaintance. The Diamond Workers' Union Building in Amsterdam makes an interesting comparison.

Bellot's motto was 'to innovate according to tradition'. He greatly admired the writings of Viollet-le-Duc, though he was less impressed by his buildings. He was strongly opposed to Le Corbusier. He was influenced by Dom Desiderius Lenz of Beuron in his theories of proportion. He was devoted to the golden section, and had a set square made in that proportion. Another Benedictine architect, Dom Hans van der Laan, was unconvinced, writing that he 'failed to see what it had to do with architecture'. Not surprisingly the ascetic van der Laan found Bellot's architecture theatrical. Later in his career Bellot made striking use of reinforced concrete. He much admired Anatole de Baudot's revolutionary church of St Jean de Montmartre (1894–1904).

The church is naturally the highlight [Figs 6.7, 6.8]. The plan is a long rectangle,

Fig 6.7. | Quarr Abbey, entrance arch to church. [Edward Diestelkamp]

Fig 6.8. | Quarr Abbey, interior of church looking west. [Edward Diestelkamp]

with a narthex for the public. The monks' choir is reached up steps, originally flanked by altars, which have been removed. Behind the side walls are narrow passages,
which have a structural function, there being no external buttressing. Pevsner
compares them with Gaudi's corridors at the convent of St Teresa at Barcelona.
The sanctuary is flanked by rectangular projections for chapels. The climax is the
vault over the sanctuary, with great intersecting arches spanning the space. The
original high altar has been removed, but the tabernacle is on the main altar in
the crypt. The refectory is spanned by arches, which give it a strong character of
its own. The reader's pulpit is of brick [Fig 6.9]. The chapter house [Fig 6.11] is
simpler, but the staircase which rises outside it has a striking rhythm of arches.

The majority of the community returned to Solesmes in 1922, after the anti-
clerical laws had been abolished in 1920, but twenty five remained. Quarr was
raised to the status of abbey in 1937. Bellot designed the library, main cloister and
the abbot's oratory at Solesmes. He was also responsible for a considerable
number of parish and monastic churches in France, the Netherlands, Belgium,
and Portugal. He died in 1944, trapped by the War in Canada, where he had gone
in 1937 to supervise the completion of the great domed Oratory of St Joseph in
Montreal, as well as building at the monastery of St-Benoît-du-Lac, Quebec.

Fig 6.9. | Quarr Abbey, refectory pulpit. [Edward Diestelkamp]

Fig 6.10. | St Hugh's Charterhouse, chapter house. [Prior of St Hugh's Charterhouse]

Fig 6.11. | Quarr Abbey, chapter house. [Edward Diestelkamp]

ACKNOWLEDGMENTS

Fr John Babeau, Prior of St Hugh's Charterhouse, gave welcome assistance. Dom Xavier Perrin, Abbot of Quarr, gave permission for a visit to the monastery and photography.

NOTES

Unless otherwise stated, information in this essay comes from the following sources. For Parkminster: *St Hugh's Charterhouse*, 1963; James Hogg, *The Carthusians: St Hugh's Charterhouse, Parkminster,* 2018. For Quarr: *Une oeuvre d'architecture moderne par Dom Paul Bellot OSB,* 1927; Dom Paul Bellot, *Propos d'un bâtisseur du Bon Dieu,* 1948 (based on lectures given in Canada in 1934); Nikolaus Pevsner, 'Quarr and Bellot', *Architectural Review,* vol. 141, April 1967, pp.307–10; Maurice Culot and Martin Meade (eds), *Dom Paul Bellot Moine Architecte,* 1996; Peter Willis, *Dom Paul Bellot, Architect and Monk,* 1996; Stewart Abbott, 'Dom Paul Bellot OSB, Twentieth Century Monk Architect and Quarr Abbey, Isle of Wight', *Ecclesiology Today,* vol.33, May 2004, pp.15–25.

1. Hogg, p.6.
2. Victoria County History, Sussex, vol.6, part 3, 1987, pp.177–82.
3. Ian Nairn and Nikolaus Pevsner, *The Buildings of England: Sussex,* 1965 edn, p.317.
4. Bellot, *Propos,* p.43.
5. Pevsner, pp.307–10.

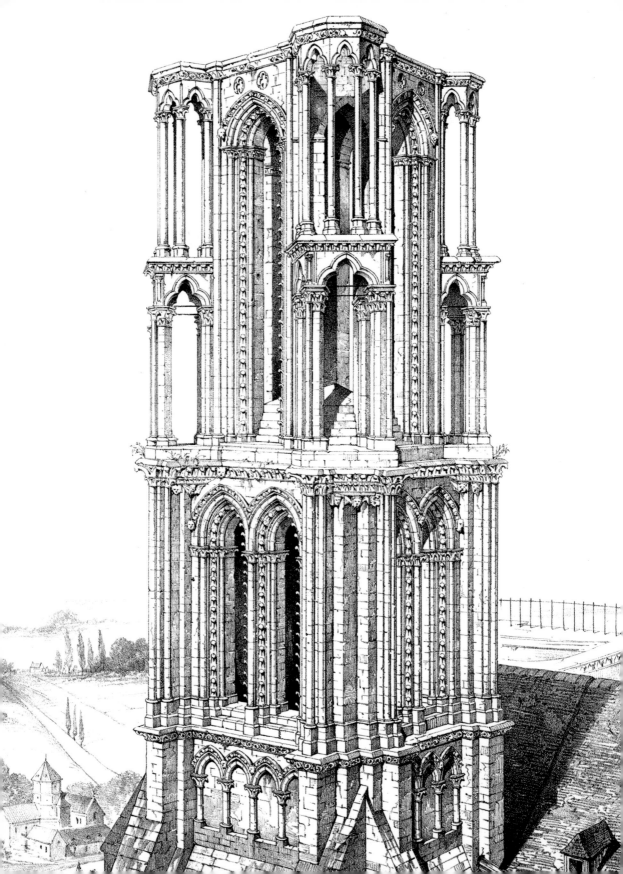

7 · French Medieval Architecture in England

ALEXANDRINA BUCHANAN

When you go abroad, begin with France. It is the great centre of Mediæval art. Perhaps the best course is to take Normandy first, as being most allied to our own country; but still more important is the district round Paris – the old royal domain – which seems to be the heart from which Gothic architecture diffused itself throughout Europe. The architecture of this central district, particularly in works of the thirteenth century, demands the closest and the most diligent study; it is the great standard and type of the style, and, without a good knowledge of it, your studies would be not only incomplete, but defective at the most vital part.[1]

So George Gilbert Scott directed the audience of the first of his Royal Academy lectures, delivered between 1857 and 1873. As Scott's words demonstrate, by the second half of the nineteenth century, the importance of France as a model was promoted, based on an understanding of its historic role. This essay aims to identify how and why this awareness arose and spread, what specific features were identified as 'French' and why they proved attractive to English architects.

Although the existence of an 'Early French phase' of the Gothic Revival has always been recognised, Joe Mordaunt Crook's 1985 article on Early French Gothic is the only dedicated study of this topic.[2] It usefully identifies the style's 'evangelists', in particular William Burges, and provides a wealth of quotations demonstrating the arguments for its adoption. The focus is primarily on texts as evidence for stylistic choice, with little analysis of how these choices manifested themselves in buildings. Most books on individual architects, such as Crook's work on Burges, or Anthony Quiney's book on Pearson, discuss their French travels and the influence these had on their design repertoire.[3] The main focus of these studies has been to locate specific influences: for example, in his work on George Edmund Street, Neil Jackson uses his sketchbooks to identify French sources for Street's church of St James the Less in buildings including St Pierre de Montmartre, the cloister and chapter house of St Georges de Boscherville and the chevet of St Jacques, Compiègne, all sketched on his 1858 sojourn in France.[4]

Starting with buildings rather than people, Gavin Stamp's pioneering article on English architects and Normandy demonstrates the appeal of the architecture of this region to English sensibilities, whilst David Brownlee's study of Street's Law Courts explores the use of French elements within that complex.[5] There has, however, been little attempt either to examine the subject holistically, asking whether particular aspects of French medieval architecture resonated most strongly with English architects, or to relate visual analysis and reproduction

Fig 7.1. | Laon Cathedral, tower attached to north transept, from W. Eden Nesfield, *Specimens of Mediaeval Architecture*, 1862.

with scholarly understanding. I therefore want to ask whether specific features of French architecture took on special significance in England because of how they were discussed in relevant literature. Furthermore, I shall argue that French architecture became familiar to English architects and their patrons through books as well as through travel. Even when source buildings can be identified, the use of their features needs to be understood in the context of their associations, which were dependent on textual as much as architectural sources.

Travel had, of course, long played an important role in architectural education and was a marker of expertise, as well as a welcome break from the heavy load of professional practice. Yet, as Burges noted, 'It is perhaps far better to study things which have been published, and which we know to be good, than to go hunting out ones less known and probably not so good, at an expense of time and travel.'[6] In this argument, books and personal sketches were valuable primarily as an *aide-mémoire*: the real requirement was to undertake detailed study of the best examples. The idea of 'good' examples, however, suggests another role played by books and other verbal discourse, for assessments of quality were neither self-evident nor static. All descriptions of the larger offices, especially those of Scott and Street, suggest febrile discussion of architectural values and the identification and use of sources. Texts, in the form of books, journalistic contributions and lectures (which were often published, or at least reported) provided a vehicle for younger men to make their name and established figures to assert their standing. Texts could make it unnecessary for architects to have visited a building to incorporate its elements into their designs. They could provide collections of specimens, both to illustrate the salient features of a style and to offer examples to copy. Identifying particular elements, either visually or textually, emphasised their significance, whilst a verbal description helped the reader to recognise them in other buildings, cogitate about them and discuss them with others. Texts thus helped to qualify what was distinctive about French buildings and why these characteristics were valuable and worthy of emulation. Nevertheless there remain aspects of buildings that were not articulated verbally.

'It seems curious that I should have been twelve years in practice, before I became acquainted with French architecture, yet I was the first among English architects, as I believe, to study it in detail in any practical way, and with practical intention.'[7] So wrote Scott, recalling a short trip to Amiens and Paris in 1847. Although he had been preceded by Pugin (father and son) and their associate, Benjamin Ferrey, and Ambrose Poynter had lived in Paris in 1830–2, Scott's assessment was largely correct as regards Goths of his own generation. Burges went to France in 1849, Street in 1850 and Butterfield by 1851 at the latest. Pearson travelled France in 1853 and Nesfield and Shaw followed them in the mid '50s. The direct influence of French medieval architecture in England therefore came relatively late. Its influence via books was, however, earlier and set the scene for later travels.

The earliest in a long series of English-language works illustrating French architecture was *Anglo-Norman Antiquities* by Andrew Ducarel, published in 1767 and focused on Normandy.[8] Ducarel was followed by a long sequence of authors, including Dawson Turner, Cotman, Pugin senior, Gally Knight, and Rickman.[9] Even before the first volume of Viollet-le-Duc's *Dictionnaire* appeared in 1854, scholarly attention had shifted towards the Ile-de-France. Recognition that the Gothic style, as defined by antiquaries, had first appeared in this region had originally been articulated by the Rev. G. D. Whittington, published in 1809. Although Robert Willis had also argued for French priority in his *Remarks on the Architecture of the Middle Ages, especially of Italy* (1835), the idea had not caught on.[10] Most architects visiting France in the mid-nineteenth century were probably under the impression that the transition from Romanesque into Gothic had taken place simultaneously across Europe, with each country following its own trajectory, although the French and English developments were generally seen to be the most vigorous. The Rev. John Louis Petit in his *Architectural Studies in France* of 1854 said as much:

> Those which have, at the time I refer to, any life or movement, at least in the direction of Northern Gothic, are the French and the English; and these, I think, may be shown to have an inherent and independent vitality of their own ... the germ of progress was in each independently and showed itself by movements in great measure independent of each other.[11]

Until the 1840s, French scholars arguing the contrary were easily dismissed by their English counterparts for dating French buildings too early, based on documentary evidence. The cathedral of Coutances, for example, was argued in France to have been built between 1030 and 1056, a statement which was manifestly absurd to English observers familiar with the stylistic table popularised by Thomas Rickman in his *Attempt to Discriminate the Styles of Architecture*.[12]

As the origins of Gothic were of the greatest interest to researchers, the priority of France in relation to later developments, notably the introduction of tracery, remained largely unrecognised. The general opinion in England was that expressed by Scott, that 'Towards the end ... of the thirteenth century [Germany, France and England] appear, by a remarkable coincidence, to have all arrived at the same point, though reaching it by different routes.'[13] His argument, based on an identification of the late thirteenth century as a universal high point of Gothic, thus favoured an international eclecticism. Although both Whittington and Willis argued that the bar tracery of Amiens Cathedral (begun 1220) was far in advance of the lancets of Salisbury Cathedral (begun in the same year), this comparison had little impact on the inclusion of specifically French forms, which tended to prefer earlier models.[14]

The Norman antiquary Arcisse de Caumont introduced Rickman's ideas to France, thus updating French antiquarian methods.[15] Just as Rickman may be credited with introducing 'Perpendicular' as a stylistic descriptor for late Gothic in England, so de Caumont introduced the term 'Flamboyant' to identify late

Gothic in France. This was first used in English by Rickman and has become a rare – if not unique – example of an architectural style being the source for an adjective now in much wider use.[16] His version of the stylistic table used 'First', 'Second' and 'Third Ogival' as labels, which provided the source for the 'First', 'Second' and 'Third Pointed' schema of the Ecclesiologists.[17]

Rickman published 'Four Letters on the Ecclesiastical Architecture of France' in *Archaeologia* (1832) and added comments on French architecture to the fourth edition of his *Attempt* in 1835, based on a tour undertaken in 1832 with William Whewell. He started to characterise French Gothic in contrast to English by noting the lack of definition of individual parts; size and number of flying buttresses; greater internal height; apsidal east end; greater distance of windows from the floor; incomplete towers; pack-saddle roofs; absence of battlemented parapets; preponderance of wheel windows; and smallness of exterior bases.[18] Petit included discussion of French examples in his *Remarks on Church Architecture* of 1841, based on extensive reading and travel, followed by the more focused *Architectural Studies in France* (1854, reprinted 1870). He had a particular interest in Romanesque architecture in the south of France and his sketches emphasised the picturesque massing/outline associated with Romanesque (Fig 7.2), the very quality Tim Mowl has identified as lacking in its contemporary reproduction.[19] Petit's work

was dismissed by *The Ecclesiologist* but extolled by Edward Augustus Freeman, whose *History of Architecture* (1849) aimed at global coverage and therefore included information on medieval France, as had Thomas Hope and would James Fergusson.[20] The German scholar Georg Moller,[21] and the second edition of Whewell's *Architectural Notes on German Churches* (1835) also touched on France. Nevertheless, their remarks were not enough to recommend France as a magnet for observing early Gothic. As

Fig 7.2. | Notre Dame de Fougeray, Cormeray. Sketch by John Louis Petit from *Architectural Studies in France*, 1854.

Scott observed, 'Oddly enough, it never occurred to me that France should be my first field of study; I knew what had been written by Whewell, Petit, and Moller, but I had not gathered this fact from what they had said.'[22]

Others who reported back with architectural information from France in the 1850s included Thomas Leverton Donaldson and James William Fraser.[23] But Robert Willis, arguably the foremost architectural historian of his generation, wrote very little specifically on French architecture, other than an article on late Gothic mouldings, which Ruskin admired but which had little practical influence.[24] In terms of specific focus on French Gothic, the most significant antiquarian scholar was Willis's publisher, John Henry Parker, who despite his fervent advocacy of the Englishness of Gothic, became something of an expert on France.[25]

Contemporary antiquarian scholarship was conveyed to a more specifically architectural audience by Scott and Street, with Street in particular adding information drawn from first-hand knowledge of French buildings. Street's work on France is now less well known than his studies of Italian and Spanish architecture, probably because it was not published in stand-alone book form.[26] Nevertheless, his advocacy of the Early French style was passionate and the arguments he proposed in its favour are representative of High Victorian aesthetics.

During the 1860s and '70s several books were published in English with drawings of French Gothic churches, catering for contemporary interest in the early French style, as well as the republication of Pugin senior's *Specimens*, by Richard Phené Spiers. These works included Nesfield's *Specimens of Mediaeval Architecture* (1862), already mentioned in Burges's approving statement, Robert J. Johnson's *Specimens of Early French Architecture* (1864), W. Galsworthy Davie's *Architectural Studies in France* (1877) and the four-volume *Study-Book of Mediaeval Architecture and Art* of Thomas Harper King (1858–68). Other works, such as Frederick Rogers' *Detail Drawings and Sketches: Measured and Drawn from Ecclesiastical and Domestic Buildings of the Middle Ages in England and France* (1868) included some French examples. Overall these works had a tendency to focus on twelfth and thirteenth-century Gothic examples, with significant interest in towers and spires and in sculptural detail. Nesfield's plates (Fig 7.1) are generally perspectival representations, including figures and genre details, there are also some examples of armoires (it is worth noting that Viollet-le-Duc's *Mobilier* was starting to appear and Nesfield, as well as his peers, designed furniture as well as buildings); Johnson and Davie had less interest in furniture but also included plans, sections, moulding profiles and orthogonally projected elevations.

As identified, the early literature had a particular interest in Normandy, and therefore in Romanesque architecture.[27] This focus was also expressed in built form, though to speak of a 'Romanesque revival', is perhaps to give coherence to a group of buildings whose variety does not merit such classification. Nevertheless, some churches in a round arched style show knowledge of the French examples. One of these, East Grafton, Wiltshire, of 1844 (Fig 7.3), was designed by Benjamin Ferrey, who had travelled with the Pugins in France. The tower, with its crocketed pyramidal roof is modelled on that of Thaon in Calvados (Fig 7.4); it has an apsidal east end and was intended to be vaulted throughout, all features characteristic of French Romanesque but less typical in England. East Grafton thus includes three of the elements which – as we shall see – came to be identified as 'French' for an English audience and well before either the 1854 publication of the first volume of Viollet-le-Duc's *Dictionnaire* or the 1855 competition for Lille Cathedral, generally considered as the starting points for the trend.[28]

Of course, the scene was set earlier, and should be associated with the scholarly interest in the origins of Gothic and its national variations outlined above. George Gilbert Scott's travels in France from 1847 were initially prompted by the descriptions of Amiens by the Dean of Ely.[29] Dean Peacock was a friend of Willis

Fig 7.3. | East Grafton Church, Wiltshire. Engraving of church by Benjamin Ferrey, sold to raise money for the building, 1844.

Fig 7.4. | St Pierre, Thaon, Calvados. [Copyright Édouard Hue, licence CC BY-SA 4.0]

and Whewell, who could have influenced his views on French architecture. Another key figure was Thomas Stevens, Rector of Bradfield, Berkshire, whose church Scott began remodelling in 1848 (and of whose views more anon). Stevens had studied at Oriel College, Oxford and was therefore within the ambit of Richard Hurrell Froude and other early members of the Oxford Society for the Promotion of the Study of Gothic Architecture. Both Whewell and Willis in Cambridge and Froude in Oxford were especially concerned with what was termed the 'Transition' from Romanesque to Gothic, a period between about 1140 and 1190. In identifying the systemic differences between Romanesque and Gothic, scholars sought to highlight the typical features of the latter, which became hallmarks of the style. This systematic analysis appealed to architectural logic and the evident working out of a system gave transitional architecture a particular fascination. As Scott put it:

> It has often been spoken of as a vice to be too fond of studying *transitional* styles. This may possibly be true as regards taking them as our models; but I hold the very contrary to be the case as to selecting them as special objects of study. They are the very periods of intellectual energy – the moments of the most intense effort of the human mind. From them we learn what zeal, what determination, what strength of will, what unity of purpose, what patient perseverance are required in working out a great good.[30]

Aside from Spiers's additions to Pugin, none of the picture books described above contain letterpress identifying the particular features of French medieval architecture, so here again we have to turn to more historical works. Parker was either alert to a nascent interest in France, or stimulated it via his 1849 *Introduction to the Study of Gothic Architecture*, whose chapter on French Gothic was based on a trip to central France earlier that year and recollections of previous visits to Normandy.[31] This highlighted a number of features of French Gothic churches, as follows:

> Larger scale and greater height than English Gothic
> Plan: apsidal east end
> Piers: 'plain round clumsy columns' rather than the clustered columns of England
> Windows: fondness for wheel windows, and later, rose windows
> Capitals: a form based on the Roman Composite or Corinthian capital; foliage less highly finished and elegant than in England
> Abaci: square form
> Mouldings: simpler than their English counterparts; square soffits or non-existent; use of crockets or foliage rather than dogtooth
> Tracery: extensive use of plate tracery; early use of bar tracery
> Doorways: heavily sculpted and often including a porch
> Buttresses: massive and bold, often with multiple flying buttresses
> West front with three doorways, surmounted by a circular window and twin towers, often with spires

Many of these features had already been highlighted by Rickman and Poynter and the list was scarcely modified by Scott in his lectures to the Royal Academy, showing that increased travel and scholarship had little effect on the intellectual framework within which such studies occurred. Scott's wide reading and magpie approach ensured that he digested current thinking for an audience of future professionals. Other authors, such as Street and Eastlake, also reinforced (without direct reference) the same list. For example, describing Pearson's Appleton le Moors church (Fig 7.5) as an exemplification of this architect's study of 'the earliest and severest type of French Gothic', Eastlake drew attention to the rounded apse, the severe and primitive carving of the capitals and the square-edged arches.[32]

A concern with transitional styles in architecture chimed with a theme, dominant from the 1840s, of 'development', evident in theology, in politics and in architecture.[33] Development meant different things to different people but the aim was to draw on historical precedent to stimulate evolution into a form properly suited to the nineteenth century. A variety of starting points for architectural development were proposed but the claims of the earliest Gothic were obvious from both a historical and an aesthetic perspective. Although the idea that Gothic had started in France was not universally accepted, architects would learn from Viollet-le-Duc and see from their travels that this was where Gothic had started its medieval development. French twelfth-century architecture could therefore offer a valid starting point for its nineteenth-century counterpart. Inspiration for architectural development could be found in English models and also Italian, and from the late 1840s the doctrine of eclecticism, proclaimed most

Fig 7.5. | Appleton-le-Moors Church, Yorkshire, west front. [Copyright Pauline E, licence CC BY-SA 2.0]

vehemently by Alexander Beresford Hope, allowed for syncretism of all historical styles. Nevertheless, given the belief that 'Gothic was the universal emanation of the mind of Christian Europe', there were clear reasons for favouring early French Gothic.[34] There were more examples of complete buildings in an early French style, meaning that they could be seen as models in terms of plan and massing as well as details. Twelfth-century Ile de France, which had never experienced the Romanesque building boom of its surrounding regions, was thus playing catch-up, resulting in many churches on every scale, from small chapels to mighty cathedrals. Some of the details in these medieval examples were mass-produced, with lathe-turned shafts and production-line mouldings. Whilst these characteristics were not discussed in relation to mechanisation by nineteenth-century architects, they might have made the style seem peculiarly well-suited to contemporary conditions. Early French architecture thus tended to be more severe than its English counterpart, with self-evident geometrical purity. Finally, Ile-de-France Gothic, with its race to ever taller elevations, with thin walls supported by flying buttresses, was more evidently engineered than either English or Italian Gothic. For architects who had imbibed Pugin's *True Principles*, French architecture would surely appear to have embodied them more clearly than English Gothic, and Viollet-le-Duc's structural rationalist arguments would have reinforced the message.

Devoid of the fussy detail that the younger men in Scott's office disliked in their master's work, the earliest Gothic had all the symbolic features that made the style appealing to the Ecclesiologists, expressed through a primitive elementalism. Burges claimed that no style of architecture could be more appropriate to the age of the railway, the battleship and democracy than an architecture characterised by 'boldness, breadth, strength, sternness and virility' – which for him was early French Gothic.

In 1859, Street stated, 'I hold the French architecture of the thirteenth century to be the noblest in Europe'. Neither he nor the great champion of English Gothic, Parker, saw any obstacle to finding inspiration in France. Parker used the argument that much of France lay within the English dominion to claim that Norman and Angevin buildings were essentially equivalent to those located in England. Street argued for the primacy of the early Gothic of the Ile de France, which lay outside the Plantagenet sphere, but 'which presents no features unsuitable for our country, or inconsistent with the demands of our climate; it is the one from the study of which I believe we should all derive an immense benefit, for it were wellnigh impossible to spend much time among the works of art which it so bountifully affords without being strongly impressed with the stern grandeur and masculine character of the men who conceived it'.[35]

Turning now to the specific features and characteristics associated with French Gothic, its height and amplitude could rarely be emulated in practice, although Street had a particular talent for emphasising internal volume, a characteristic of Continental churches he much admired.[36] Street also made extensive use of apsidal east ends, although, as we have seen, these had a long ancestry in England.

Their association with France is evident in the use of an apse in Scott's revised designs for Exeter College Chapel, Oxford (1848, built 1854–60), which includes Rayonnant windows of very tall proportions [Frontispiece], comparable with those of the upper chapel of the Sainte Chapelle which he had recently visited, although the use of tierceron vaults is more typically English.[37] In the later 1850s there was much discussion of the origin of the typically French chevet, with an apse and a continuous run of chapels accessed by an ambulatory, in the pages of *The Ecclesiologist*. This was spurred by a review of James Fergusson's *Illustrated Handbook of Architecture*, first published in 1855, which outlined the development of the apse and ambulatory plan and its evolution into the continuous chevet in terms close to modern understanding of the subject.[38]

A dichotomy was thus set up between the Continental preference for apsidal terminations (already highlighted by Rickman and Parker) and the English use of the square east end, meaning that any use of the former after around 1855 was making a consciously Continentalist choice, whilst an angled apse was probably seen as particularly French. Conversely, Butterfield's preference for square east ends was deliberately Anglicising. Nevertheless, there was a significant difference between the function of the ambulatory in Victorian churches and in their medieval predecessors. In the Middle Ages the ambulatory was primarily used for accessing the ring of chapels surrounding the hemicycle. In Anglican churches there was no need for numerous subordinate altars, so this element of the plan was omitted, a very un-medieval arrangement which left the ambulatory to function, as its contemporary nomenclature suggests, as a 'procession path', for the more elaborate liturgy promoted by the ritualists.

Another plan derived largely from France which became particularly popular in England was the wide nave with narrow aisles, rising to the full height of the main vessel and performing a buttressing role, typified by Albi Cathedral and the churches of the Cordeliers and the Jacobins in Toulouse. Though reproduced in texts, this arrangement seems to have been adopted from personal contact. Whether the model was as invariably French as has sometimes been implied can be challenged, as there were also examples in Spain, and Bodley's use of this plan type at St Augustine's, Pendlebury (1875), was clearly derived from the church of the Dominicans in Ghent.[39] Moreover, churches with similar – but by no means identical – arrangements involving very narrow aisles include the early example of Clutton's St Jude's, Bethnal Green (1842–6, demolished); later came Street's, All Saints', Clifton, Bristol (1864), and Pearson's, St Augustine's, Kilburn (1871–7). Quiney has identified the direct influence of Albi on Pearson's designs for St Augustine's, Kilburn, and John Thomas has traced a succession of progeny either looking directly towards the Continental examples or via secondary inspiration.[40] The popularity of this plan may have been its ability to accommodate large congregations without the impediment of piers.

The buttressing within the aisles of these Albi-influenced churches enabled the construction of stone vaults, another feature associated with French architecture. Tim Mowl suggested that the collapse of the nave vaults at Ferrey's East Grafton in 1842 caused the premature death not only of the visiting clergyman George Augustus Montgomery but also of the Romanesque revival, and aborted the revival of vaults in England.[41] This may be something of an over-statement, but it is true that the Camdenian and Puginian preference for the early fourteenth-century English parish church as a model limited the scope for vaulting in the early years of the Gothic Revival as the source buildings usually had timber roofs. After the early twelfth century, vaulting in the main spans of English parish churches is exceptional, whereas in France it was *comme il faut*. However the turn to Continental models created a new vogue for stone and brick vaults, particularly over the chancel, marking this area out as having particular sacred significance. An early example, which may have been intended to recall early French precedents, is Scott's 1848 design for Thomas Stevens at Bradfield (Fig 7.6). It can be hard to identify whether architects had in mind French or Italian models, as the two have few distinguishing characteristics, although the rare use of sexpartite vaults (e.g. over the choir of Pearson's St Peter's, Vauxhall), would link more closely to French prototypes than to Italian.

Fig 7.6. | Bradfield Church, Berkshire, interior.

When we look more closely at Victorian vaults, we see that they rarely bore a very close relationship to medieval examples in either three-dimensional form or construction techniques. For example, Viollet-le-Duc identified a distinction between French and English coursing patterns in vault webs (Fig 7.7). In France, the coursing for the overwhelming majority of webbing was designed to end with a straight line parallel to the ridge, whereas in England the pattern of coursing usually ended with a jagged junction at the ridge.[42] In the so-called 'French' method, the different curvatures of the diagonals and bounding arches meant that the stones could not simply be laid in parallel lines. Instead, each course of stones was slightly tapered, allowing the angle of the coursing to be adjusted as it rose, creating a smooth transition from bottom to top. In Victorian vaults, the use of bricks or standardised stone blocks in the webbing did not allow for 'French' unconformities, so an angular junction at the ridge is the norm. In his Royal Academy lectures, Scott described the national differences and noted: 'The French seem much offended by the appearance of the English system; and I remember feeling in the same way when I first saw the French method. The latter seems to throw undue pressure on the diagonal ribs, while the English mode appears to throw it more equally on *all*

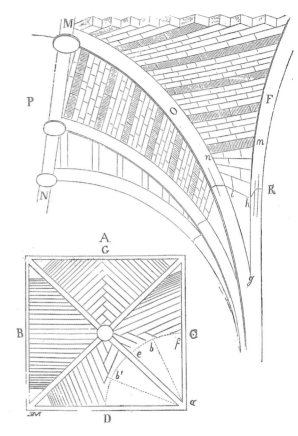

Fig 7.7. | Diagram of English vaults, from Viollet-le-Duc, *Dictionnaire raisonné de l'architecture*.

the ribs; throwing it, in fact, down into the direction of their meeting-point'.[43]

In French models, sexpartite vaulting is normally found in conjunction with a system of alternating supports, although in Notre-Dame de Paris we find it used above an arcade of columnar piers. Columnar piers are very frequently found in Victorian Gothic, deriving ultimately from the Roman columns Abbot Suger used in his choir at Saint-Denis and identified with French Gothic by Parker. Alternating supports are also not unknown – for example in the Episcopal Cathedral in Edinburgh, a late design by Scott. They have been described as following the New Shoreham model, but Scott would have been aware that New Shoreham and its Victorian progeny had another common ancestor in Canterbury Cathedral, where he was then working on a design for new choir stalls.[44] Canterbury's alternating pier system was part of the work of the French master, William of Sens, whose design had been discussed in detail by Robert Willis. The use of an early French style in the Anglican mother church might therefore have been a strong factor in its use by Scott in the cathedral of the Scottish capital.

Along with vaults, spires were viewed as essential to the Gothic style, defined by Whewell as the embodiment of an Idea: 'vertical, aspiring, indefinite'. In his *Architectural Notes on German Churches*, Whewell noted, 'the transition from the unmixed Romanesque, which English and French writers generally call Norman, to that style of Early Gothic which we know so well under the name of Early English, may be traced best perhaps in the towers of churches in Normandy'.[45]

Fig 7.8. | Noyon Cathedral, Salle du Trésor from east. [Copyright Richard Plant]

Fig 7.9. | Mantes Cathedral, interior looking east. [Copyright Pierre Poschadel, licence CC BY-SA 4.0)]

The importance of towers and spires in Normandy was reiterated by Parker, who gave a paper on the subject of St Etienne in Caen to the Royal Institute of British Architects (partially reproduced in the 1874 edition of Pugin's *Specimens*). Parker argued that the presence of stone decoration in the form of shingles in the spires of Normandy suggested that the stone spires were intended as non-combustible replicas of wooden predecessors. He also claimed that the continuous line of development of spires in the region was evidence of an indigenous evolution, thereafter exported across Europe.[46] He identified as the starting point, the pyramidal roof of Thaon (Fig 7.4) and traced a sequence of examples from the locality culminating in the octagonal spire with spire lights. As we have seen, Thaon had already provided inspiration for Ferrey at East Grafton, whilst Stamp and others have identified a number of Victorian spires apparently indebted to French models. As well as the octagonal form, the saddleback tower noted by

Fig 7.10. | Red House, Bexleyheath. [Copyright Ethan Doyle Wight, licence CC BY-SA 3.0]

Rickman was another spire-like feature more commonly found in France than in England, albeit with enough English precedents to be acceptable to an architect like Butterfield. Besides its stark geometry, the saddleback tower might have had the benefit of being cheaper or easier to erect than a conventional spire, as it did not require shaped masonry.

The use of 'plate' tracery was also more likely to follow French models than English, simply because there are more of them. This is again a feature whose revival in practice should be seen in relation to contemporary scholarship. Plate tracery – that is to say where complex window designs are formed as groups of openings within large slabs of stone, rather than a single opening being subdivided by moulded bars of stone – was rare, if not unknown in revival architecture prior to the 1850s, which is not surprising, because plate tracery as a phenomenon was not conceptualised before 1849. In that year, Willis gave a lecture to the Royal Archaeological Institute on Salisbury Cathedral, which has plate tracery in its triforium and bar tracery in the cloister and chapter house – Willis coined both terms to describe the differences between them. Although Willis's lecture remained unpublished until 1972, his usual publisher, Parker, discussed the terms in his *Introduction to the Study of Gothic Architecture* of 1849, as part of a discussion of whether tracery was imported from the Continent or home-grown.

Rickman, Poynter, Parker and Scott identified wheel windows as a favourite French feature. They had also been a common feature in Romanesque revival churches and could suggest Italian inspiration, but some examples have a strongly French flavour, as for example the western rose of Pearson's Appleton-le-Moors Church already mentioned, which seems to have been based on the east window of the Treasury at Noyon Cathedral (Fig 7.8). The openings of the triforium grouped within a single arch and the round openings of the apse of Mantes Cathedral have been identified as influences on the fenestration of Philip Webb's Red House (Figs 7.9, 7.10). In 1858 Webb had travelled to France with William Morris and Charles Faulkner and admired the 'gaunt amplitude' of Mantes, which he later compared with Noah's Ark.[47]

Fig 7.11. | St Fin Barre's Cathedral, Cork, west front. [Copyright Wikipedysta, licence CC BY 2.5]

Fig 7.12. | St Fin Barre's Cathedral, foolish virgins from west front. [Wikimedia, Public Domain]

Museum. Clutton was the Secretary of the Museum's committee and other Early French enthusiasts offered support to the institution via donations and lectures, although Street expressed concerns that its holdings might encourage sculptors to copy historic examples directly rather than 'conventionalising' from nature. The Architectural Museum became a centre for debates about the nature of architectural sculpture in the Gothic Revival. Until such time as sculptors could conventionalise for themselves, early French Gothic offered as a solution the 'crocket capital', as used by Street in the church of St Paul's, Herne Hill (1858), Bodley in St Michael's, Brighton (1859–62) and Scott in the Mill Road cemetery chapel – these were the 'conventionalised Corinthian' capitals highlighted by *The Ecclesiologist*.[60]

French mouldings were also more easily replicated by nineteenth-century carvers than contemporary English examples. Later architectural historians characterised French Gothic as being based on thin wall construction, making arch mouldings correspondingly shallower than those in England, where the thick walls of Romanesque construction remained the norm.[61] Whereas English masons used their thick walls as the opportunity for luxuriant series of rolls and hollows, French voussoirs were restricted to rolls and hollows at the angles, with a flat face in between. This allowed a clear correspondence between arch orders and any pier shafts, again offering a constructional logic appealing to advocates of 'true principles'.

Transactions of the Exeter Diocesan Architectural Society, vol.5, 1856, pp.108–13.

24. R. Willis, 'On the Characteristic Interpenetrations of the Flamboyant Style', *Transactions of the Royal Institute of British Architects*, vol.1, no.2, 1842, pp.81–7. See also Elena de Andrés, Elena Pliego, and Alberto Sanjurjo Álvarez, 'Robert Willis' Contribution to Understanding the Gothic Flamboyant Style', *Proceedings of the First Conference of the Construction History Society*, 2014, pp.343–53.

25. See the following papers by J. H. Parker in *Archaeologia*: 'Notes made during a Tour in the West of France', vol.34, no.2, 1852, pp.273–95; 'Continuation of Observations on the Ancient Churches in the West of France', vol.35. no.1, 1853, pp.34–47; 'Third Letter … upon the Ancient Churches in the West of France', vol.35, no.2, 1854, pp.359–67; 'Medieval Architecture in Aquitaine', vol.36, no.2, pp.1-13; 'Medieval Architecture in Aquitaine; in continuation and conclusion of previous Papers', vol.36, no.2. 1855, pp.311–25. Also by Parker: 'The Abbey Churches at Caen', *Gentleman's Magazine*, vol.214, 1863, pp.283–301, 412–25; 'On the Abbey Churches at Caen, with Illustrations', *Papers read at the Royal Institute of British Architects*, 1862–4, pp.99–126; 'On the Church of St Stephen or the "Abbaye aux Hommes", at Caen', *ibid.*, 1865–6, pp.89–96.

26. G. E. Street, 'Architectural Notes in France I', *The Ecclesiologist*, vol.19, n.s.16, 1858, pp.362–72; 'Architectural Notes in France II', *ibid.*, vol.20, n.s.17, 1859, pp.18–26; 'Architectural Notes in France III', *ibid.*, vol.20, n.s.17, 1859, pp.91–100; 'Architectural Notes in France IV', *ibid.* vol.20, n.s.17, 1859, pp.178–84; 'Architectural Notes in France V', *ibid.*, vol.20, n.s.17, 1859, pp.332–40. An unpublished notebook of Street's on France was edited and published by Georgiana Goddard King, *Unpublished Notes and Reprinted Papers*, Publications of the Hispanic Society of America, vol. 100, 1916 (also at https://www.gutenberg.org/ebooks/58450).

27. Tina Waldeier Bizzarro, *Romanesque Architectural Criticism: A Prehistory*, 1992.

28. Charles Eastlake, *A History of the Gothic Revival*, 1872, p.319; H.-R. Hitchcock, 'High Victorian Gothic', (p.53); *idem*, 'G. E. Street in the 1850s', *Journal of the Society of Architectural Historians*, vol.19, no.4, 1960, pp.145–71 (p.158); Crook, 'Early French Gothic', p.49.

29. Scott, *Recollections*, p.146.

30. Scott, *Lectures*, p.131.

31. J. H. Parker, *Introduction to the Study of Gothic Architecture*, 1849, preface.

32. Eastlake, p.303.

33. David B. Brownlee, 'The First High Victorians: British Architectural Theory in the 1840s', *Architectura*, vol.15, 1985, pp.33–46; Michael Hall, 'What Do Victorian Churches Mean? Symbolism and Sacramentalism in Anglican Church Architecture, 1850–1870', *Journal of the Society of Architectural Historians*, vol.59, no.1, 2000, pp.78–95.

34. Review of James Fergusson's *Illustrated Handbook of Architecture* in *Saturday Review*, 26 January 1856, p.236.

35. Street, 'Architectural Notes I', pp.363–4.

36. G. E. Street, 'The True Principles of Gothic Architecture and the Possibility of Development', *The Ecclesiologist*, pp.247–62 (p.256); Andrew Saint, *Richard Norman Shaw*, 2010 edn, p.25.

37. Geoffrey Tyack, 'Gilbert Scott and the Chapel of Exeter College, Oxford', *Architectural History*, vol.50, 2007, pp.125–48.

38. 'Fergusson's Handbook of Architecture', *The Ecclesiologist*, 17, n.s. 14, 1856, pp.23–31.

39. Michael Hall, *George Frederick Bodley and the Later Gothic Revival in Britain and America*, 2014, p.171.

40. John Thomas, 'The influence of Albi Cathedral: the use of historic precedent in nineteenth and twentieth century church design', *The Journal of Architecture*, vol.3, no.2, 1998, pp.85–105; *idem*, 'The "Beginnings of a Noble Pile": Liverpool Cathedral's Lady Chapel (1904-10)', *Architectural History*, vol.48, 2005, pp.257–90.

41. Mowl, p.47.

42. Eugène Viollet-le-Duc, *Dictionnaire raisonné de l'architecture française*, vol. 4.

43. Scott, *Lectures*, p.195.

44. Peter Howell and Ian Sutton (eds), *The Faber Guide to Victorian Churches*, 1989, p.40.

45. W. Whewell, *Architectural Notes on German Churches*, 1835 edn, pp.202–3.

46. Parker, 'On the Church of St Stephen'.

47. Philip Webb to W.R. Lethaby, 16 May 1905, in John Aplin (ed.), *The Letters of Philip Webb, vol. 4, 1903-1914*, 2016, p.154.

48. I am grateful to Nicholas Olsberg for discussion of this point.

49. A. Poynter, 'On the Contemporary Styles of Gothic in England and France', *Transactions of the Royal Institute of British Architects*, vol.1, 1842, p.74.

50. Scott, *Recollections*, p.155.

51. Eastlake, p.319.

52. Scott, *Recollections*, p.202.

53. Meredith Cohen, *The Sainte Chapelle and the Construction of Sacral Monarchy*, 2015, p.87.

54. Scott, *Recollections*, p.204.

55. *Ibid.*, p.205.

56. Poynter, 'Contemporary Styles', p.79.

57. Victorian Web, https://victorianweb.org/sculpture/architectural/108.html.

58. For the Architectural Museum, see A. C. Buchanan, 'The Royal Architectural Museum, 1851–1917', unpublished M.Sc. thesis, Bartlett School of Architecture, University College London, 1991; Edward Bottoms, 'The Royal Architectural Museum in the light of new documentary evidence', *Journal of the History of Collections*, vol.19, no.1, 2007, pp.115–39; Isabelle Flour, 'On the Formation of a National Museum of Architecture: The Architectural Museum versus the South Kensington Museum', *Architectural History*, vol.51, 2008, pp.211–38.

59. G.E. Street, 'Architectural Notes I', p.367.

60. For one of many statements on 'conventionalism', see J. P. Seddon, 'Conventionalism in Ornament', *Civil Engineer and Architect's Journal*, vol.25, 1 Sept 1862), pp.273–6.

61. The classic exposition of Gothic being the result of a desire to combine thin wall construction with vaulting is Jean Bony, *French Gothic Architecture of the 12th and 13th Centuries*, 1983. See review by Stephen Murray in *Art Bulletin*, vol.69, no.2, 1987, pp.300–2.

62. Eastlake, p.131.

63. G. E. Street, 'Architectural Notes I', p.363.

64. *Idem*, 'Architectural Notes V', p.340.

8 · Eugène Viollet-le-Duc and the English: Admirers and Detractors

GILLES MAURY

Since the research carried out at the end of the 1970s for the celebration of the centenary of Eugène Viollet-le-Duc's death, his immense work has not ceased to be reassessed. The recent bicentenary and the unfortunate fire at Notre-Dame de Paris have once again focused attention on this key figure of nineteenth-century European architecture and prompted new investigations.

Robin Middleton, in his excellent paper published in 1980 in the proceedings of the colloquium held in Paris,[1] already explained in great detail the complexity and extent of Viollet-le-Duc's relations with his British counterparts, but since then, no significant research had made it possible to organise, amplify or clarify this information. Now that more archives are accessible, knowledge of the Victorian and French architectural scene of the Second Empire has been considerably expanded. For this essay, all of Viollet-le-Duc's foreign correspondence has been consulted,[2] classified, and then compared with the archives of the RIBA and the Victoria and Albert Museum in particular. This is an opportunity to summarise several years of work and to review what has been discovered.[3]

This implies presenting not a chronology, but a sort of picture, a hierarchical classification of the types of relations that the eminent French architect maintained not only with his English colleagues, but also with scholars and archaeologists. In the following account, the protagonists will be presented somewhat like members of a game of 'Happy Families', from the most distant to the closest, from friends to enemies. Viollet-le-Duc's English relations will be characterised by the nature of the exchanges that animated them, and will highlight several aspects of his influence in Great Britain.

ENGLAND AND VIOLLET-LE-DUC

Before starting this portrait gallery, it is necessary to introduce what England meant to Viollet-le-Duc (1814–79) [Fig 8.1]. In 1850, at the age of 36, Viollet-le-Duc travelled to England for three weeks with his friend Prosper Mérimée, 'inspecteur général des monuments historiques en France' and a famous writer, a man of the world with a vast network of contacts. The two men visited the Parliament under construction, but apparently did not meet either Charles Barry or A. W. N. Pugin. They also went to Westminster Abbey and made various excursions to Ely, Peterborough, Lincoln [Fig 8.2], Salisbury, to mention the main sites.[4] From

Fig 8.1. | Eugène Viollet-le-Duc. Photograph by Nadar

Fig 8.2. | Lincoln Cathedral, 'Chevet', drawn by Viollet-le-Duc in 1850. [Médiathèque du Patrimoine, Fonds Viollet-le-Duc, album Ecole Anglo-Normande]

this trip, Viollet-le-Duc retained various points that were to leave a deep impression on him and that were to be found in his written works, such as the famous *Dictionnaire raisonné de l'architecture*,[5] where, for example, English carpentry is given several rather impressive pages. This influence also became manifest in his own architectural designs, but that is another subject.

From this first encounter with England and from all the exchanges that followed, Viollet-le-Duc developed a deep admiration for English architecture, but also for the pragmatism and efficiency of his colleagues, and this was to continue until the end of his life. It is the country by far the most often cited in his dictionaries, with Germany coming second – not always for architectural qualities.[6] Viollet-le-Duc's interest and curiosity about England is another matter, as is what he saw and what he learned there. But it is not surprising that this led to a consequent development of his relationships with British colleagues, and through his writings and fame, to various types of influence on English architecture and decoration.

A WIDE CIRCLE OF ADMIRERS

Generally speaking, it was the members of the Royal Institute of British Architects who did the most to promote Viollet-le-Duc in Great Britain. In the 1850s and 1860s, personalities such as Thomas Donaldson and Frederick Pepys Cockerell were dominant inside this institution. As soon as the *Dictionnaire raisonné* was published and immediately distributed in Britain (1854), admiration was widespread, and the formal letters exchanged between the three men, although merely courteous, also testified to an exchange of ideas.[7] Though the largely classical orientation of Donaldson and Cockerell was at odds with the preoccupations of the French architect, this nascent admiration would grow. Viollet-le-Duc was first appointed an honorary member and foreign correspondent at the end of the Paris World Exhibition (1855), and was finally awarded the RIBA Gold Medal in 1864. At this stage Viollet-le-Duc's works as opposed to his books had no direct influence in England. But when in 1874 R. Phené Spiers lectured to the RIBA about Pierrefonds, showing printed copies of the restoration drawings [Fig. 8.3] which he had acquired some months before when visiting the castle, some members were inclined to be critical of his restoration methods, though others were enthusiastic and supportive.[8] From this verbal joust, Viollet-le-Duc appears more as a trigger than an influencer.

Matthew Digby Wyatt was one of the first enthusiasts for the *Dictionnaire raisonné*, and his passion led him immediately after the publication of the first volumes to consider translating them. He wrote to Viollet-le-Duc in 1855, but also to publishers, and enquired about the cost of renting woodcuts for the illustrations.[9] Given the size of the task, and perhaps also given certain editorial difficulties, Wyatt did not pursue this idea and we do not know what he thought of the French architect's work.

If we follow William Burges' remark, 'we all crib from Viollet-le-Duc',[10] it is

Fig 8.3. | Pierrefonds Castle, lithographic elevation, coloured in. A complete set of these lithographs in the possession of Phené Spiers was shown during a debate at the RIBA in 1874. [Victoria & Albert Museum, Prints and Drawings, E.6093–1906]

not always easy to find concrete proof. In itself, the influence of Viollet-le-Duc on a whole generation of architects would require a very detailed study of hundreds of buildings. Happily, there are a few telling traces of the fascination that the French architect had for younger colleagues. John Pollard Seddon is one of these, although his name has not so far appeared in the list of architects under his spell. He copied Viollet-le-Duc, once again his *Dictionnaire raisonné*, if not to take direct inspiration from it, at least to extend his decorative repertoire [Fig 8.4]. The drawings Seddon made from the *Dictionnaire* are significant evidence of a form of reception of the French architect's work, even on a modest scale.[11]

Other admirers included the trio of Anthony Salvin, William Eden Nesfield and Richard Norman Shaw. One can only briefly summarise here a perfect example of a rather indirect relationship, which nevertheless testifies to a fascination that left some traces. Salvin seems never to have corresponded with Viollet-le-Duc. However, they might have actually met at the 1855 World Exhibition in Paris, where Salvin saw Viollet-le-Duc's drawings on Carcassonne, which left a strong impression on him.[12] Salvin himself exhibited an enormous model of Peckforton Castle, the only model of its kind on display at the time, and therefore remarkable. Following this crossover, coincidental or otherwise, Salvin was more or less forced to draw inspiration from the restoration works in Carcassonne for those he was to do at Windsor Castle, on commission from Prince Albert.[13]

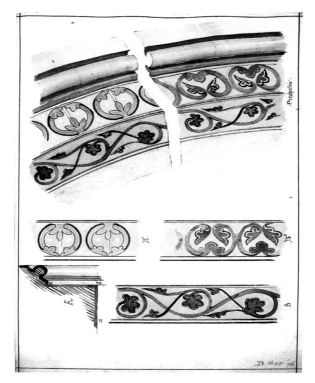

Fig 8.4. | Watercolour by J. P. Seddon, copied from *Painting* entry in the *Dictionnaire raisonné de l'architecture*, vol.VII, p.85. [Victoria & Albert Museum, Seddon archives, Prints and Drawings, D.1648]

By a curious mirror effect, Viollet-le-Duc would offer a free interpretation of the keep at Warkworth Castle in the second volume of his *Entretiens* in 1872. Despite the fact that this building was fitted out by Salvin in 1866, there does not appear to have been any exchange between the two men.[14] Salvin's nephew, the young Nesfield, and his friend, Shaw, were drawn into the discovery of Viollet-le-Duc's restoration work on the great cathedrals during their many trips to France. Nesfield approached Viollet-le-Duc at least twice, and Viollet-le-Duc must have helped him, for in a letter of 1857 from Donaldson we read : 'Nesfield, the young man for whom you have been so kind'.[15] Perhaps it was permission to visit construction sites? A trace of this remains in Shaw's drawings, published in 1858; at Amiens, Shaw draws not just the cathedral but also the Viollet-le-Duc building site [Fig 8.5].[16]

Alfred Waterhouse's architecture is a case in point, partly because of the influence of Viollet-le-Duc's theoretical writings, but also in terms of decorative arts. Waterhouse owned a bench [Fig 8.6], the shape of which seems to have been inspired by some of the French architect's drawings, but the history of which is still a mystery: its presence in the collections of the Château de Compiègne, following a gift from the Waterhouse family, is not well documented by the archives.[17]

Fig 8.5. | View of Amiens Cathedral, showing the building site and workshop by Viollet-le-Duc, from Richard Norman Shaw, *Architectural Sketches from the Continent*, 1858

Fig 8.6. | Bench after Viollet-le-Duc (or an original design), bought by Alfred Waterhouse in 1878 and now in the Musée Napoléon III, Palais de Compiègne. [Photograph, RMN-Grand Palais (domaine de Compiègne)/ Stéphane Maréchalle]

Within this group, however, we have to distinguish two categories, those who were scholars but whose personality encouraged friendship, and those with whom the exchanges were more informative or professional. The level of influence of Viollet-le-Duc is more limited, or more diffuse, because it concerns above all the exchange of archaeological knowledge and the advancement of knowledge about medieval architecture.

John Henry Parker, the famous publisher and archaeologist, was the English scholar closest to Viollet-le-Duc, and spoke French perfectly. While there is no doubt that his *Glossary* had a real influence on Viollet-le-Duc,[18] in return, in the small amount of correspondence that has come down to us (running from 1850 to 1867), it seems that Parker very often relies on Viollet-le-Duc's advice, obviously with regard to French architecture, but also to its influence on English architecture, especially during and after the so-called Norman period. Parker also regularly depends on Viollet-le-Duc's recommendations for visits during his many journeys to France. He directs the scholar towards a certain type of building, thus influencing what he looked at and how it might be interpreted.[19] The mutual esteem that can be read in the words of their letters offers us a wholly admirable and encouraging example of Franco-English collaboration.

Further on the topic of scholarly relations, mention must be made of Professor Robert Willis, with whom Viollet-le-Duc had some exchanges of views, at least indirectly. There is no existing correspondence between the two men, but this does not mean that such letters did not exist. Certainly, Parker acted as an intermediary between Willis and Viollet-le-Duc in some of his letters. It is clear from what Viollet-le-Duc says about Willis's texts on English vaults that the benefit was mutual [Fig 8.7].[20]

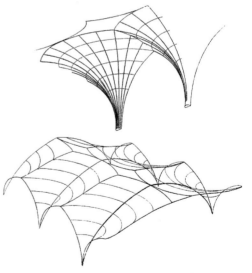

On a more concrete, professional level, Viollet-le-Duc is in contact with some very minor figures in the English architectural scene, although it is not easy to clarify the origin of the contacts. Charles Edward Davis, an architect in Bath, wrote several times to Viollet-le-Duc in 1868, asking for advice on the restoration of churches in the Cotswolds.[21] This little-known story, which it is not possible to document further on the French side, deserves following up, as it might reveal aspects of the impact of Viollet-le-Duc's thinking on restoration in England. It seems, in the only letter that has come down to us, that the questions were essentially technical.

Fig 8.7. | Part of *Construction* entry from the *Dictionnaire raisonné de l'architecture*, vol.IV, p.122, quoting Willis' book on medieval vaulting.

Among the famous names of Victorian architecture, two stand out, but for almost opposite reasons. The first is George Gilbert Scott, prolific both as a restorer and as an architect involved in the modernity of his time. Could Scott be claimed as Viollet-le-Duc's distant half-brother?

Scott and Viollet-le-Duc were exact contemporaries, and their careers developed in parallel, with similar intensity. As a matter of course, Viollet-le-Duc is regularly compared to George Gilbert Scott, a leading figure of the English neo-Gothic period, a great creator as well as restorer, someone whose output was enormous and who managed a very important office at the time. Scott and Viollet-le-Duc must surely have met several times in person. The first time, though there is no evidence for it,[22] would have been during the Frenchman's trip to England in 1850, the second in 1855 at the Paris Exposition Universelle. Viollet-le-Duc was in charge of the admissions committee for the architecture section, and it is significant that England was the most represented nation. It is not surprising that Donaldson, Cockerell, Scott etc., men he knew, were included. Scott and Viollet-le-Duc received medals at the final ceremonies. The 1855 Exposition offered an implicit confrontation between the two architect-restorers, as the new high altar of Clermont-Ferrand Cathedral was presented, all gleaming with its new gilding, while in the architecture section could be seen the drawings of the high altar of Scott's Ely Cathedral. The designs were very different but nevertheless one feels that both architects were in control of their sources and in the modern management of the Gothic. At Ely, Scott was in charge of work very similar to that of Viollet-le-Duc in Notre-Dame de Paris or Amiens: consolidation, repair, partial dismantling, refurbishment, rearrangement of stalls, etc. Like him, he was in charge of many of the great English cathedrals. One can understand Viollet-le-Duc's desire on occasions to dismantle seventeenth and eighteenth-century changes, when he saw that in England they did not hesitate to complete medieval stalls with a new screen, like Scott's at Ely and elsewhere.

The parallel careers of the two men is really a subject in itself, because there are many signs of a reciprocal influence, albeit a measured one, perfectly integrated on each side within strong professional practices based on sound principles. Scott admired Viollet-le-Duc's modern creations, such as the new sacristy at Notre-Dame which he was able to visit,[23] and although Viollet-le-Duc did not comment on the work of Scott which he was able to see, it is amazing how many issues they dealt with at the same time and in sometimes comparable ways, such as the introduction of metal into contemporary Gothic architecture.

THE CLOSEST ENEMY?

The nature of the relationship between William Burges and Viollet-le-Duc could be described as one of love-hate, or, to hijack a famous song, one might use the formula: *je t'aime, moi non plus* (I love you/me neither).[24] From reading J. Mordaunt Crook's texts, it is clear that Burges admired Viollet-le-Duc in many ways, and that he might have dreamed of writing something comparable to the *Dictionnaire raisonné*. At the same time, it is quite understandable that their two very different ways of working were a hindrance to a possible rapprochement or even a friendly understanding.

Indirect contacts between the two men are numerous, and it is impossible for Viollet-le-Duc not to have come across Burges' work at various events or in the journals of the time. This began with the competition for Lille Cathedral, which Burges won with Henry Clutton in 1856. Burges also visited Amiens several times during Viollet-le-Duc's restoration project in the 1850s. In fact, more than Scott, Burges could have claimed a better relationship with the French architect. He probably borrowed the most from Viollet-le-Duc's drawings, which are easily identifiable in his work, as Crook himself points out,[25] but his frequent visits to to the French architect's buildings and works were doubtless also to the point.

The case of Pierrefonds is particularly symptomatic of an influence that does not want to speak its name, and of an element of bad faith maintained by a kind of jealousy. Burges, who visited Pierrefonds in the 1860s, denied Viollet-le-Duc the quality of being a true architect, wanting to acknowledge only his qualities as a scholar or a savant.[26] He made his visit in the middle of a very unfinished project, for which the financial means could not be compared with Burges' extraordinary budgets. Deliberately, or through ignorance, he refused to put the contexts of Viollet-le-Duc's creations into perspective with his own. This did not prevent him from borrowing important features from Pierrefonds, such as the idea of the seated monstrous figures, the staircase on a hexagonal plan with a central pillar, etc. It is difficult today, from the French point of view, to agree with Mordaunt Crook's peremptory conclusion that Viollet-le-Duc for Burges was 'a great scholar, an average architect, and a disastrous restorer', to which he adds: 'posterity has confirmed this verdict'.[27] These words, written in 1981, but still present in the revised 2013 version of Crook's handsome book, have been refuted by years of research in France on the importance of Viollet-le-Duc's work, both as architect, designer and restorer.

For Burges, as for Scott, it would require a great deal of work to discover, point by point, what Viollet-le-Duc was able to contribute to their professional and creative careers and to establish a precise chronology for it, in particular with regard to Burges' visits to France and the rhythm of his publications.

THE FAITHFUL FRIEND

At the top of the hierarchy, no other English architect was more influenced by Viollet-le-Duc than Benjamin Bucknall. As an architect, Bucknall occupies a subordinate position in Victorian architecture, but this does not mean that he was not talented. Discreet as he was, unquestionably very independent in his practice, and not particularly in search of recognition, he could have remained an obscure architect,[28] working away from the limelight in Gloucestershire and Wales. His disappearance into voluntary exile in Algeria after 1874 on grounds of health also added to Bucknall's lack of status in England.

Bucknall successively went through all possible stages of relationship. At first a distant admirer, then an arm's-length pupil, next a zealous disciple and ardent defender, and finally a friend. This astonishing journey, despite the geographical distance and the age difference, bears witness to a real sharing of ideas that was to begin and develop from 1852 onwards, only to end with the death of the two architects.[29]

Only seven letters from Bucknall to Viollet-le-Duc have survived, but this remains the most extensive correspondence with an English architect preserved, and there is no doubt, given the content of some of these letters, that there were others, probably lost. To correspond regularly does not necessarily mean to be influenced. But in the exceptional case of Bucknall, he was to find in Viollet-le-Duc's thinking and achievements a true mirror to his own concerns.

It is clear that the two met many times. According to current research it was Bucknall among English architects who had the most contact with Viollet-le-Duc, including being invited to his most intimate retreat, the chalet La Vedette in Lausanne, in 1876.[30]

Bucknall seems to have discovered the first two volumes of the *Dictionnaire raisonné* as soon as they appeared, in 1854 and 1856. Between these publications, from 1855 onwards, Charles Hansom, Bucknall's former master and employer, was commissioned by William Leigh to build a large house on his land near Stroud, in Gloucestershire. Initially led by Hansom, the project and the building site were gradually left in the hands of Bucknall alone. The result was the shell, never finished, of Woodchester Park [Fig 8.8].[31]

Fig 8.8. | Woodchester Park, view of unfinished interior. Benjamin Bucknall, architect, 1855–72. [Author's photograph]

The conjunction of the discovery of the *Dictionnaire* with the questions posed by the Hansom office's projects and sites is probably a powerful trigger. This had a regular and increasingly intense impact on Bucknall's entire career. Bucknall's first documented project dates back to 1857 and all his future work developed in parallel with Viollet-le-Duc's publications. The first meeting between the two men took place in 1862; it was Bucknall who came to Paris, to make a few visits, but above all to discuss architecture and show Viollet-le-Duc the plans of Woodchester, which they discussed.[32]

Woodchester Park is indeed full of references to the *Dictionnaire raisonné*. Firstly, the general order of the building, whose structure is entirely in stone, and the management of the arches and inner buttresses in particular, reveal a careful reading of the corresponding pages in the *Dictionnaire*. Secondly, a whole series of details, from the capitals of the columns to the gargoyles, not forgetting other sculpted elements, such as the finials, were clearly copied from certain drawings by Viollet-le-Duc [Figs 8.9, 8.10].

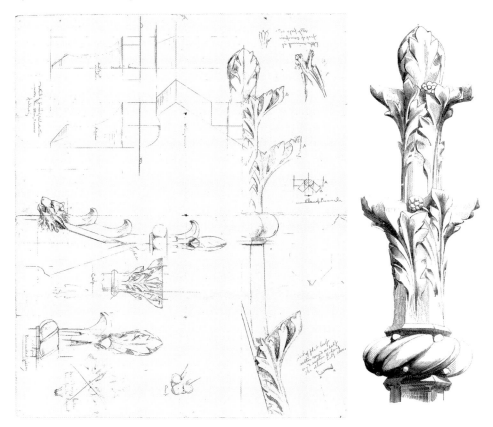

Fig 8.9, 8.10 | Left, drawing by Benjamin Bucknall for the chapel finials at Woodchester. [Gloucestershire Archives, D12263-82abg] Right, one of the finials in the *Fleuron* entry in the *Dictionnaire raisonné de l'architecture*, vol.V, p.478.

When he planned a second visit to France for the summer of 1869, Bucknall was no longer a student seeking help or advice with his projects, but an established architect. The tone of the correspondence, while certainly deferential, evolves towards more sharing. Viollet-le-Duc seems to have greatly facilitated Bucknall's stay, giving him access to the Pierrefonds building site for almost a week, and showing him the model of the Notre-Dame spire and the unexecuted drawings for Saint-Pierre-de-Chaillot, Paris. Ideas were also shared. Bucknall was on a perpetual quest: 'I am always seeking to discover the principles', he wrote to Viollet-le-Duc, adding: 'I believe I have found many of the principles with which I notice you always proceed and which I know are the substance of art'.[33]

The impact of this second trip and these visits is palpable in a series of works Bucknall was building at this time in Wales. The choices made for the extension to the Old Grammar School, Swansea, in 1869 echo the nobility of Pierrefonds. The large superimposed rooms of this school, including the one on the top floor with its overturned ship's hull vault, entirely painted in small compartments, the powerful colour scheme throughout, the fireplaces and their heraldic motifs make these rooms one of the most immediate applications of Viollet-le-Duc's work.[34]

It was, however, thanks to Bucknall that Viollet-le-Duc's ideas were able to penetrate widely in Great Britain, as he was their principal and most zealous translator. The first complete book by Viollet-le-Duc to appear in Britain was *How to build a house, an architectural novelette* (*Histoire d'une maison*, 1873), translated by Bucknall and published in 1874. This first educational novel by the French architect is imbued with an English spirit, paradoxically demonstrating the degree of penetration of British principles and lessons in what was intended to be a French model of construction and architecture. No doubt that made the book easier to translate and get published, as the illustrations could easily be transposed to the English landscape [Fig 8.11]. Remarkably, the second design for the Leigh family that Bucknall proposed in 1874 when he hoped to take over Woodchester Park is simply an adaptation of a design published in this book [Fig 8.12].

The sequence of translations obviously implies a close relationship, since they appeared at shorter intervals: *Annals of a Fortress* came out in 1875, *The Habitations of Man in all Ages* in 1876, the two volumes of *Lectures on Architecture* in 1877, the same year as the book on Mont Blanc. Bucknall is therefore both the transmitter of ideas and the most skilful practitioner of Viollet-le-Duc's principles – suggesting that the latter's integration into the Victorian architectural milieu was perfectly possible.

In concluding this essay, it is necessary to raise a question that would require further serious research and gathering of information. I have focused here mainly on the English architects and scholars who had more or less direct contact with Viollet-le-Duc, and also with his built work. However, Viollet-le-Duc's influence on the English seems to have spread beyond these scholarly circles to an initiated public of enthusiasts for Gothic and for art in general. For instance William Leigh, Bucknall's client at Woodchester, had at least one copy

Fig 8.11 | Elevation of garden front of house for Mr. Paul, from Viollet-le-Duc, *Histoire d'une maison*, 1873, fig.29.

Fig 8.12 | Perspective sketch by Benjamin Bucknall of new house to be built at Woodchester Park, 1874. [Liz Davenport, *Why Was Woodchester Mansion Never Finished?*, 2010]

of the *Dictionnaire raisonné* in his library, perhaps bought on the advice of the Hansoms, which may explain the direction in which his house project developed. Another family, the Gibbs of Tyntesfield, had not only the two Viollet-le-Duc dictionaries, but also some of his educational novels, which are still on the library shelves. Was young Anthony Gibbs so impressed by the *Dictionnaire raisonné du mobilier* illustrations as a child that he commissioned an extraordinary bronze and crystal chair (*c.*1877) copied from a Viollet-le-Duc design as an adult – or even children's beds and other furniture?[35] He visited France for the first time in 1869, but what did he see? Pierrefonds, like many tourists of that time? How many others might have shared these two families' fascination for Viollet-le-Duc's writings and designs?[36] That is an investigation for the future.

Can we conclude from all this that Viollet-le-Duc was influential in England? Unquestionably yes, because fame implies different forms and intensity of influence. A simple comparison offers a final glimpse of the prominent place that Viollet-le-Duc occupies in England. Among the RIBA Gold Medals awarded to French architects during the Victorian period, who can rival Viollet-le-Duc in terms of aura, presence in debates, and dissemination of thought through his writings ? Jacques-Ignace Hittorff in 1855? The more traditional Jean-Baptiste Lesueur in 1861? Charles Texier, obscurer, in 1867? Joseph-Louis Duc, more discreet, in 1876 ? I exclude the Marquis de Vogüé, a scholar, who was awarded the medal in 1879. Only Charles Garnier, recipient in 1886, equals Viollet-le-Duc in fame, but was he influential in as many fields as the latter ? César Daly, architect and well-known editor of the *Revue générale de l'architecture et des travaux publics*, a close friend of Viollet-le-Duc, received the gold medal in 1892. Is this not a form of homage to a school of thought that Viollet-le-Duc had defended so well ? The talents of the architects thus honoured need not be disputed. But none equals Viollet-le-Duc in terms of his influence on English soil, whether in terms of ideas, writings or the positive or negative reception of his architectural works.

NOTES

1. Robin Middleton, 'Viollet-le-Duc: son influence en Angleterre', in *Actes du Colloque international Viollet-le-Duc, Paris 1980*, 1982, pp.263–83.
2. Preserved at the Médiathèque du Patrimoine, Charenton-le-Pont, Fonds Viollet-le-Duc: hereafter MDP, FVLD.
3. This essay is based on research carried out as part of a *habilitation* or higher academic qualification, to be presented in 2022 as *Viollet-le-Duc et l'Angleterre. Recherches et échanges autour de l'habitation et du gothique moderne*, under the supervision of Jean-Philippe Garric, Université Paris Panthéon-Sorbonne.

4. All these drawings are kept in the Médiathèque du Patrimoine, Charenton-le-Pont, Fonds Viollet-le-Duc, album 'école anglo-normande', 2021/024/54.
5. Eugène Viollet-le-Duc, *Dictionnaire raisonné de l'architecture française*, 10 volumes, 1854–68.
6. My research has determined that although Germany is more often cited in terms of buildings, the presence of England is dominant in terms of iconography (very large engravings) and also of bibliographic references.
7. Examples in MDP, FVLD include Donaldson's letters : N°88 (1856) 2012/024/004, and N°174 (1857) 2012/024/004.

8. R. Phené Spiers, 'On the château of Pierrefonds, and its restoration by M. Viollet-le-Duc', in *RIBA Transactions*, session 1873–4, 1st series, vol. 24, pp.54–65.

9. MDP, FVLD, letter N°14 (1855) 2012/024/004.

10. Quoted by Middleton, p.279.

11. Victoria & Albert Museum, Seddon archives, 7 sheets. The drawings are taken from the article on Painting in the *Dictionnaire*.

12. Jill Allibone, *Anthony Salvin, Pioneer of Gothic Revival Architecture*, 1988, p.68.

13. *Ibid.*, pp.145–6.

14. Eugène Viollet-le-Duc, *Entretiens sur l'architecture*, vol.2, 1872, pp.490–5. Warkworth Keep had been published in *Some Account of Domestic Architecture in England,* by T. Hudson Turner and J. H. Parker, vol.III, 1859, a book Viollet-le-Duc possessed.

15. MDP, FVLD, letter N°6 (1858?) 2012/024/04.

16. Richard Norman Shaw, *Architectural Sketches from the Continent*, 1858.

17. Palais de Compiègne, documentation department. Two letters accompany the gift from Waterhouse's daughter, but are not entirely clear on the origin of the bench, which is directly attributed to Viollet-le-Duc.

18. Martin Bressani, *Architecture and the Historical Imagination. Eugène-Emmanuel Viollet-le-Duc, 1814–1879*, 2014, pp.230–3.

19. MDP, FVLD, letter N°439-40 (1850) 2012/024/03.

20. The article in *Dictionnaire* vol.9 on vaults, pp.523–36 in particular, includes a number of drawings by Willis, who is described as a 'learned teacher' who has done 'remarkable work'.

21. MDP, FVLD, letter n°726 (1868) 20212/024/07.

22. There is a letter from Scott to Viollet-le-Duc, which does not confirm that they met: MDP, FVLD, letter N°411 (1850) 2012/024/03.

23. Scott regularly visited France, and very often Viollet-le-Duc's restoration sites. See Gavin Stamp, *Gothic for the Steam Age, an Illustrated Biography of George Gilbert Scott*, 2015, p.57.

24. Song by Serge Gainsbourg, performed with Jane Birkin, 1969.

25. J. Mordaunt Crook, *Willam Burges and the High Victorian Dream*, revised edition, 2013.

26. *The Builder*, 20 Dec 1873, p.1001.

27. Crook, p.94.

28. There has been little academic research on Bucknall. One article of a biographical nature has been published: Stephen Bucknall, 'Benjamin Bucknall, disciple of Viollet-le-Duc and his brothers Robert and Alfred', in *Minerva*, vol.2, 1994, pp.8–14.

29. Gilles Maury, 'Benjamin Bucknall (1833-1895). Admirateur, élève, disciple, ami', Proceedings of the Symposium, *Les éléves de Viollet-le-Duc*, Paris, 2020: to be published.

30. MDP, FVLD, letter n°273–74 (1875) 2012/024/014.

31. Mark Girouard, *The Victorian Country House*, 1985 edn, pp.188–93.

32. MDP, FVLD, letter n°671 (1862) 2012/024/005.

33. *Ibid.,* letter n°98 (1869) 2012/024/008.

34. The building was published by Viollet-le-Duc. See Benjamin Bucknall, 'Nouvelles constructions annexes à l'école de Swansea', *Encyclopédie d'architecture*, 2nd series, 1873, vol.II, p.29.

35. James Miller, *Fertile Fortune, the Story of Tyntesfield*, National Trust, 2003, pp.116–8.

36. Viollet-le-Duc's works can be found in several private home libraries: see the online inventory of the National Trust collections.

9 · From Mewès and Davis to Blow and Billerey: Histories of Beaux-Arts Teaching and Architectural Practice between France and England

ANTONIO BRUCCULERI

During the first two decades of the twentieth century, an interest in French architecture mediated through attention to the teaching system of the Ecole des Beaux-Arts, grew in England, especially London. As a means of understanding influences *of* and resistances *to* French architectural culture in England, it is interesting to try to interpret the contribution of two Anglo-French professional partnerships, Charles Frédéric Mewès and Arthur Joseph Davis, and Fernand Billerey and Detmar Jellings Blow. Both were highly invested in teaching and practice of architecture. With Mewès, Davis directed the first Beaux-Arts Atelier created in 1912 in London, and shortly thereafter Billerey also imported the French atelier teaching methods to England. Nevertheless an overview of the architectural practice of both partnerships shows that during the Edwardian years their buildings already expressed the tension between a growing Beaux-Arts compositional approach and the dominance of English traditions and the Arts and Crafts Movement.

BIOGRAPHIES

Two of the quartet of protagonists in this essay are French, the other two are British; three of them were very close to the French Beaux-Arts pedagogical system.

The oldest is Charles Frédéric Mewès (1858–1914). Born in Strasbourg, he was the son of a merchant, Frédéric Mewès, and Julie Sophie Laure Schützenberger, of a Jewish family from the Baltic which was forced to leave Alsace because of the Prussian invasion and opted for France in 1872. He had been a student in the architecture section of the Ecole des Beaux-Arts in Paris. Trained in the atelier of Jean-Louis Pascal, which he joined on 25 February 1878, he reached the second stage of the Grand Prix de Rome competition in 1881, 1882 and 1884, and he was *logiste* in 1885, the year in which he graduated.[1] Mewès probably met Arthur Davis in Paris during the second half of the 1890s, following which he was active in France and London. He represented the spread of classicist eclecticism throughout Europe, practising with colleagues in different countries.

Fig 9.1. | Staircase at 10 Carlton House Terrace, London. Blow and Billerey, architects, 1906 [Historic England Archive, BL20223]

Arthur Davis (1878–1951) was not French, but he studied architecture in Paris. Born in London, the son of a businessman of Jewish origin, he was taken as a child by his father with his family to Brussels. Davis was among those who at the end of the nineteenth century went to study at the Ecole des Beaux-Arts.[2] He was a student in the *atelier préparatoire* of Jules Godefroy and Eugène Freynet; he applied for admission in February and June 1894, and was finally admitted to the second class in May 1895. One of the particular ways in which Davis learnt his architecture was through the practice of circulation, competition and exchange of drawings between students. That is shown in particular by the photographs of drawings that atelier comrades like Louis Faure-Dujarric and Paul Davis offered him.[3] Moving to the atelier of one of the most important French architects of the time, Jean-Louis Pascal, where Mewès had previously trained, Davis passed into the first class in 1896. His last 'mention' at the Ecole des Beaux-Arts dates from May 1898.[4]

Born the same year as Davis, Louis André Fernand Billerey (1878–1951) concentrated his architectural activity on the British side of the Channel.[5] No student records from the Ecole des Beaux-Arts about him remain. Though defined in 1965 by Nikolaus Pevsner as a 'Beaux-Arts trained Frenchman', Billerey never attended the official *section d'architecture* of the Ecole. He was born at Louvier near Rouen; his father was a departmental architect of the Eure. When twelve, Billerey was sent to a family in England to learn English. At the age of eighteen he was studying architecture in Paris. He himself later gave the impression of having been at the Ecole des Beaux-Arts. He displays a first-hand experience of one of the ateliers in Paris, and in a talk given at the RIBA in 1913,[6] he alludes to conversations with the architect Henri-Paul Nénot, winner of the Grand Prix de Rome in 1877. As Nénot was one of the closest pupils of Pascal,[7] this suggests that Billerey too may have been in Pascal's atelier. In 1900 he travelled in Italy, and there he met the British architect Detmar Jellings Blow (1867–1939). By September 1902 Billerey was in London in Blow's office, where he was working for him as an assistant; a partnership between the two dated from 1905.

Younger than Mewès but older than Davis and Billerey, Blow is the only one of the four who had no contact with the Ecole des Beaux-Arts. Born in London, he was the son of Jellings Blow, a City of London merchant. He was educated at Hawtreys School, Slough, and at South Kensington School of Art, where in 1883 he formed a long-standing friendship with his fellow student Edwin Lutyens, who was two years his junior.[8] In 1885 he began his training at the firm Wilson, Son & Aldwinckle, where he remained for four years, and attended the Architectural Association starting from 1887.[9] He won both the Association's Silver Medal and Travelling Scholarship and the Royal Academy's Silver Medal and travelling Scholarship. He then undertook a long study trip to the continent, initially with Sydney Cockerell.[10] In 1888, at Abbeville in northern France, they met John Ruskin, who took an interest in their studies and then took Blow on a first journey in Italy in the autumn and winter of 1889.[11] On his return to London, Blow worked with the art dealer Arthur Collie. At the same time, he met some architects and

Arts and Crafts designers such as Sydney Barnsley, Reginald Blomfield, Ernest Gimson, William Richard Lethaby, William Morris and John Sedding. On Ruskin's advice, he spent nearly a year with a working mason in Newcastle-upon-Tyne, learning the practical business of building[12] before completing his training with Philip Webb and supervising with him the repair and restoration of East Knoyle Church (1891–3).[13] In 1892 Blow won the Pugin Prize and was admitted to the Art Workers' Guild.[14] Blow's practice before 1906 had been almost exclusively in the country.[15] No. 28 South Street, on the Grosvenor estate in London (1902–3), was the only notable exception. Between 1906 and 1914 most of the Blow and Billerey partnership's commissions were in the West End of London, where Blow had become close to the 2nd Duke of Westminster, the rich magnate who owned the Grosvenor estate.

THE RISE OF BEAUX-ARTS TEACHING IN LONDON

In the years during which the activity of the two partnerships – Mewès and Davis, and Blow and Billerey – grew, a strong interest in French architectural culture developed in London, in particular relation to the teaching of architecture at the Ecole des Beaux-Arts in Paris.[16]

Starting in the 1870s and 1880s, in particular at the Architectural Association where Blow himself had studied, Richard Phené Spiers, followed by Lawrence Harvey, endeavoured to introduce the pedagogical methods and modalities specific to the Ecole des Beaux-Arts across the Channel. A few attempts were made, notably by Frank T. Baggallay and Walter Millard, to introduce Beaux-Arts-style atelier teaching.[17] In due course the AA experimented with models for centralizing education, linking training and professional practice, in ways consistent with the efforts towards regulating teaching and professional reorganization carried out by the Board of Architectural Education, created in 1903 by the RIBA.[18]

The beginning of the twentieth century was a turning point. In 1903 the editors of the *Architectural Review*, investigating training practices, asked Julien Guadet, professor of architectural theory at the Ecole des Beaux-Arts (1894–1908), to write an article on the subject, at just the time he was publishing his four-volume work, *Éléments et théorie de l'architecture*.[19] The article drew readers' particular attention to the atelier teaching system as the main peculiarity of the Beaux-Arts method, Guadet having himself directed an atelier from 1871 to 1894. The following year, the *Architectural Review* also published the drawings of the project by Ernest Hébrard, winner of the Grand Prix de Rome, as well as a school project by a French student, Raymond Rousselot.[20] In the years immediately following, the RIBA awarded the Royal Gold Medal to French architects like Honoré Daumet in 1908 and Jean-Louis Pascal in 1914.[21]

Over the course of the first decade of the twentieth century, the Beaux-Arts model won a dominant place in the Architectural Association too. Starting from their own Parisian experience, Day School students such as Henry Philip Cart de Lafontaine described in the pages of the *AA Journal* how the Ecole des Beaux-Arts teaching worked.[22] In 1913 for the first time a British architect, although of American origin, Howard Robertson, graduated from the Ecole after having completed all studies in the second and first class [Fig 9.2].[23] Philip Dalton Hepworth, among the last students of the Architectural Association Day School to leave for Paris on the eve of the First World War, even obtained, in 1914, the Rome Prize, established in 1912 as a British equivalent to the Grand Prix de Rome.[24]

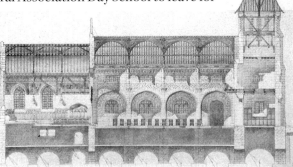

Fig 9.2. | Diploma project of 1913 by Howard Robertson for a church for Anglican worship, long section. [*Bulletin hebdomadaire de la SADG*, 1913, Société française des architectes, Paris]

Meanwhile the RIBA had exhibited in 1908 the drawings of Selinunte in Sicily by Jean Hulot, winner of the Grand Prix de Rome.[25] In 1913 Reginald Blomfield could recall his fascination, during his visit to the Parisian *Salon d'architecture*, for the drawings of 'restorations' as, for example, the Altis at Olympia by Victor Laloux, exhibited in 1885. Contradicting the 'critics of the Ecole des Beaux-Arts' who thought that 'this kind of work was not a very good preparation for practical architecture', he stressed the benefits of the study of 'some of the greatest remains of antiquity' and asserted that 'studies of this kind filled the mind with ideas of a high standard'.[26]

The years 1904–14 therefore marked a real triumph for the Beaux-Arts teaching model in the British capital. During this time, twenty-five students, almost all from London, went to Paris to study architecture. Most of these were British, though Howard Robertson was originally from the United States and Francis Swales from Canada.[27] Of these at least eight officially entered the Ecole des Beaux-Arts, not counting those who had only attended *ateliers préparatoires*.[28] Of course, the acceleration of the approach to the French educational system cannot be separated from the political and cultural framework of the Entente Cordiale between France and Britain, signed on 8 April 1904. But it also reflected a specific interest that had steadily grown between the second half of the nineteenth and the beginning of the twentieth centuries, with particular reference to the atelier teaching system.[29]

Ten years later, on 17 March 1913, during a talk he gave at the RIBA on 'French Modern Architecture', Billerey identified very precisely the challenges of teaching in the atelier, a term he translated in English with the word 'studio', emphasizing the role played by the atelier master towards the pupils, but also the relationships between the pupils themselves:

> To my mind, the greatest and most important tradition followed by French students is that tradition of working in common in a studio under the guidance of a master. The studio keeps alive the experience gained by previous generations, and each generation adds to that experience the benefit of its own, supersedes

slowly out-of-date methods or fits them to newer requirements. The master has himself been in the studio in his younger days, has obtained the degrees and successes which students are now seeking for, and offers them the benefit of the experience he has himself acquired by his work, his travels, and his achievement in practice. But, perhaps, still more than by the influence of the master, the young student will benefit by the experience gained by his companions who have been in the studio a few years before him.[30]

In fact the first formal example of the atelier system did not exist in London until 1912, when a Beaux-Arts Committee created within the Society of Architects established a 'First Atelier of Architecture'.[31] Arthur Davis was its master, assisted by two French architects: Charles Mewès and Jean-Paul Chaurès. This initiative obtained the support of the French educational and professional community. Great atelier masters such as Jean-Louis Pascal or Victor Laloux lent their names to the patronage committee of the First Atelier. The Société des architectes diplômés par le Gouvernement also gave its support via its president, Alphonse Defrasse, and his vice-president, Jules Godefroy, testifying to the significance attached by this French official body to the link between training and profession through the delivery of a diploma.[32] During 1912–13 contacts and exchanges between London and Paris multiplied: French architects offered their assistance to Davis, such as Jacques Gustave Félix Ravazé or Louis Faure-Dujarric; others like Jules Godefroy visited the new London atelier.[33]

The format of the First Atelier was modelled on Beaux-Arts practice, even in shaping the project exercises as competitions.[34] 'Medal-winning' drawings were given an important role as a pedagogical tool. That is related to the practice of emulation fostered in the atelier, with the system of school competitions as the pivot.[35] This explains the place given in London, from the early 1910s, to drawings of student projects from the Ecole des Beaux-Arts as specimens to be exhibited and published, representing an exemplary pedagogical approach for the British students, in particular in the First London Atelier.[36]

FOLLOWING THE BEAUX-ARTS MODEL FROM TEACHING TO BUILDING

Over and above the impact of this approach to teaching, the English interest in the composition and language of French architecture, especially that of Paris, can be detected by analysing some London buildings realized from the early years of the twentieth century, first of all by the masters of the First Atelier: Davis and Mewès.

Helped by Arthur Davis for the drawings, Mewès had been ranked fourth in the 1898 competition for the Grand and Petit Palais of the 1900 International Exhibition in Paris. As part of this event, he realized the project for the Palais d'Économie Sociale et des Congrès.[37] He was the author of projects for some *hôtels particuliers* in Paris and also for a building, carried out between 1912 and 1914, at 68 Avenue des Champs-Élysées for the perfumers Jacques and Pierre Guerlain. His interest in specimens of monumental and classical composition had already appeared at the turn of the century, particularly in the field of large houses

Fig 9.3. | Château de Porgès, Rochefort-en-Yvelines, from the air. Charles Frédéric Mewès, architect, 1899–1904. [Wikipedia Commons]

Fig 9.4. | Drawing Room at Polesden Lacey. Mewès and Davis, architects, 1906, perhaps using old panelling. [National Trust]

outside Paris, such as the castle he built between 1899 and 1904 at Rochefort-en-Yvelines for Jules Porgès [Fig 9.3].[38] Working with Davis, Mewès brought his interest in the elegance of French classicism to bear on the remodelling of two English country houses, Luton Hoo and Polesden Lacey. In the latter, a plainish building of the 1820s was transformed with Louis XV-style interiors [Fig 9.4].[39]

In addition, Mewès applied a Beaux-Arts eclectic language in public buildings, as shown also by his Parisian projects, especially the Crédit Foncier, Rue Cambon, of 1912.[40] This is to the fore in his projects abroad: the architecture of banks in Belgium, Zurich and Basel. But above all, it is clearly recognizable in the architecture of hotels. In Madrid, Mewès with Luis de Landecho designed the Ritz Hotel (1906–10), while in a series of hotel projects in London, Mewès with Davis completed the interior of the Carlton Hotel, altered the Hyde Park Hotel and went on to carry out the entirely new Ritz Hotel (1904–6) [Fig 9.5].[41] In all these projects Mewès and Davis combined skill in composition of plan with mastery of the French classical style for the elevations. On the eve of the opening of the First Atelier, this mastery was clearly evident in the façade of the Royal Automobile Club [Fig 9.6], built between 1908 and 1911.[42] In the headquarters of the Morning Post (1906–7), Mewès & Davis successfully integrated a composition on a half-open plot with a façade design in the traditions of Haussmann [Fig 9.7].[43]

Fig 9.5. | Ritz Hotel under construction, 1905. [*Fireproof Magazine*, October 1905]

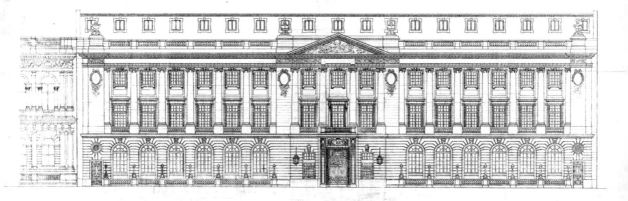

Fig 9.6. | Royal Automobile Club, elevation to Pall Mall. Mewès and Davis architects, 1908-11. [RIBA Archives, 69222-3]

Fig 9.7. | The Aldwych, London, in 1908, with Morning Post Building to left. Mewès and Davis architects, 1906–7. [Historic England Archive, BL20208]

The partnership of Blow and Billerey turned for inspiration to the French tradition in a different way, at any rate in London.[44] This is evident from some extensive interior embellishments, as at 10 Carlton House Terrace [Fig 9.1] or at the Avenue Theatre, Northumberland Avenue [Fig 9.8].[45] It is especially true for two urban mansions executed on the Grosvenor estate: 44–50 Park Street and 37–38 Upper Grosvenor Street in 1911–12 [Fig 9.9], and the façade of 46 Grosvenor Street in 1910–11 [Fig 9.10] both very different in manner from Blow's earlier 28 South Street. Billerey's hand is evident in both, particularly the façade of 44–50 Park Street.[46]

Indeed, it was in relation to public architecture that Billerey first argued in his RIBA lecture of 1913 for the primacy of contemporary French architecture. Its prototype could be dated back to Charles Garnier's project for the Opéra – an example of the 'perfect type of modern planning',[47] as Richard Phené Spiers had already emphasized in the 1860s, as had Lawrence Harvey in his private correspondence with his brother and in articles published in *The Builder*.[48] This also involved, as Billerey said, 'absolute sincerity in distributing the masses so as to express their purpose, joined to a perfect classical unity in the grouping of these masses.'[49] He also focused on examples closer to the present, from the Sorbonne building by Nénot, to the Grand and Petit Palais for the International Exhibition of 1900, which 'frankly illustrate this return to the classical tradition'[50] and the addition to the Bibliothèque Nationale by Pascal.

Billerey nevertheless gave the example of the Château du Doux in Corrèze, built to designs by Pascal [Fig 9.11]: according to him this castle 'would not be out of place in Scotland'.[51] This example allowed Billerey to argue that 'monumental

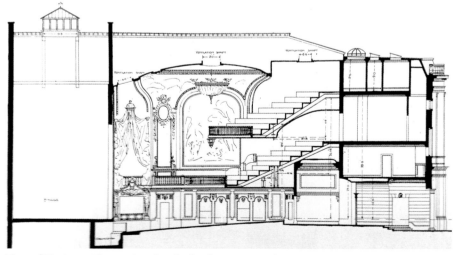

Fig 9.8. | Playhouse Theatre, Northumberland Avenue, London, section.
Blow and Billerey, architects. [*Architectural Review*, January 1906]

Fig 9.9. | 44–50 Park Street and 37–38 Upper Grosvenor Street, Mayfair, in 1912. Blow and Billerey, architects, 1911–12. [Historic England Archive, BL21872]

Fig 9.10. | 46 Grosvenor Street, Mayfair, front in 1924. Blow and Billerey, architects, 1910–11. [Historic England Archive, CC001642]

town architecture does not prevent architects treating country domestic architecture in a spirit similar to the British conception of it'.[52] Naturally perhaps, it was on the topic of country-house architecture that serious differences between English and French architectural culture arose, for example in Edward Warren's reaction to Billerey's talk:

> We had much to learn from France in thoroughness of training, and in the convinced acceptance of a contemporary manner. France [...] might aptly take lessons of us in individuality and elasticity of expression, and the sympathetic handling of detail. There was a marked tendency at this moment, begotten of our admiration for things French, to copy as exactly as possible, and without any translation as it were, French architectural fashions, and to do our streets and squares with Franco-Greek elevations. That was a pity and an absurdity. If one must be Greek, if one must adopt a windowless, chimney-less, stairless manner of building, evolved from hard material and a brilliant climate by the alien needs of an alien race, and apply it to the much-windowed, much-chimneyed, infinitely staircased requirements, to the soft dull skies and soft dull materials of Great Britain, was it necessary to seek the transposition at second hand? '*Autre pays, autres mœurs*.' If we must be Greek, let us be Anglo-Greek on our own lines, and pay to our brilliant neighbour the better and more intelligent compliment of imitating her ideals and her methods, rather than making imitative travesties of her achievement.[53]

Fig 9.11. | Château du Doux, Altillac, Corrèze. Jean-Louis Pascal. architect, 1904–6. [www.chateaududoux.com]

According to Warren, the lesson to be learned from the French teaching methods was undeniable, but British architects should not fall into a sterile stylistic imitation, and France should in turn take a lesson from typical characteristics of architectural design and execution in England. Assimilating rather than imitating French modes of teaching was also claimed as the aim in the prospectus presenting the First London atelier.[54] Even a partisan of French classicism like Reginald Blomfield, in relation to a high school project in London inspired by the Beaux-Arts model, expressed his puzzlement about its passive assimilation in England.[55]

Blomfield pointed to two opposite approaches to architectural design coexisting at the same time. Reacting to Billerey's RIBA talk, he alluded to the architecture of the recently built Musée Galliéra in Paris, 'one of the most beautifully designed buildings of modern times and representing very truly the best French treatment of classical architecture'.[56] But as regards Billerey's example of the Château du Doux by Pascal, Blomfield did not hesitate to point out the weaknesses of the French approach to designing country houses. 'One knew to look for a house that seemed all fireworks', commented Blomfield, adding: 'In this respect ... we might claim something for England; we had the sense of the quietly picturesque.'

It is not surprising, given the differences in architectural training evident in the case of Blow and Billerey, to see the divergence between the house at 46 Grosvenor Street, which they conceived together, and some of their projects during the years of the Great War, such as Hilles House, Painswick, Gloucestershire, or Broome Park, Barham, Kent. At Painswick [Fig 9.12], Blow designed and built himself a country house in the traditional Cotswold manner, into which he moved in January 1917.[57] When Billerey went off to become an officer in the French army, serving as an interpreter, one of the few remaining commissions left for Blow was the restoration and embellishment of a country house near Canterbury, Broom Park, originally of 1635–8, which he remodelled for Lord Kitchener.[58]

Fig 9.12. | Hilles House, Painswick, Gloucestershire. Blow and Billerey, architects, 1914–17. [www.hilleshouse.co.uk]

CONCLUSION

However, we must ask how far Arts and Crafts visions and Beaux-Arts visions of architectural design can really be considered as disconnected or even conflicting in the years 1900–1914. Responding to Billerey's RIBA talk in 1913, Edward Warren said:

> I was fortunate enough to have several friends amongst French architects, and they all generously and cheerfully conceded the palm to England for domestic buildings. They frequently, indeed, expressed unbounded admiration for the ingenuity of plan, the quiet harmony of exteriors, and the dignified comfort of interiors. '*Le comfort anglais*' as exemplified by modern English houses won their admiration, and they expressed perpetual surprise at the care and thought by our architects upon even minute details. '*Vous dessinez jusqu'aux clous des portes*', said a French architect to me the other day.[59]

Can we talk about an integrated process of assimilation stimulated by the Franco-British cultural exchanges of those years, in which the work of two firms considered is especially revealing? When we look at the attention paid by Mewès and Davis to interior design down to furniture details, even if it is in a Louis XV style,[60] we can perhaps observe a rival approach in the other direction, and a genuine attempt to transplant and infuse a French look to the British context.

The final gesture in these attempts at transcultural exchanges was an exhibition of architecture opened in May 1914 in the Pavillon du Jeu de Paume attached to the Louvre.[61] In particular, the aim of this Anglo-French architectural exhibition was to relate contemporary production in England both to its historical heritage and to architectural teaching, combining modernity and 'the solid tradition of Classic', never really lost in England, as Blomfield claimed in his preface to the exhibition catalogue.[62] At the same time, British architectural education, from the Royal Academy School to the First Atelier created in London, was compared to pedagogical practices of the *section d'architecture* of the Ecole des Beaux-Arts and a selection of drawings of the French school was included in the exhibition.[63] In the end, training appeared as the most fruitful means of assimilation of French architectural culture into England. This trend was tragically interrupted, like so much else, by the First World War.

NOTES

1. See the biographical file by Marie-Laure Crosnier-Leconte, in *Dictionnaire des élèves architectes de l'École des beaux-arts (1800–1968)*.

2. Richard Chafee, *The teaching of architecture at the École des Beaux-Arts and its influence in Britain and America*, PhD, University of London (Courtauld Institute), 1983, 2 vols, vol.1, pp.346–9.

3. For example, see the photographs of a school project for a private mansion, Arthur Davis photographic archives, RIBA Archives, SD160 (27). Original drawings kept in the Collections of the ENSBA (Ecole nationale supérieure des Beaux-Arts), PJ 2435.

4. Crosnier-Leconte.

5. Chafee, vol.1, pp.319–20.

6. *Journal of the Royal Institute of British Architects,* 29 March 1913, pp.317–38.

7. See Albert Louvet, 'Paul-Henri Nénot (1853–1934)', *L'Architecture*, 1935, no.7, pp.241–4; also Crosnier-Leconte.

8. Gavin Stamp, *Edwin Lutyens Country Houses*, 2001, p.11.

9. Architectural Association Archives, Nomination Papers, boxes F501–506.

10. For Cockerell, see Michael Drury, *Wandering Architects: In Pursuit of an Arts and Crafts Ideal*, 2000, pp.5–26.

11. On Detmar Blow's excursions between 1891 and 1896, Drury, pp.27–43.

12. Drury, p.36, n. 22.

13. On Blow's relationship with William Morris and Philip Webb, see Michael Drury, 'William Morris and Philip Webb: Their Influence on Detmar Blow and the Wandering Architects', in Chris Miele (ed.), *From William Morris. Building conservation and the Arts and Crafts Cult of Authenticity, 1877–1939*, 2005, pp.159–86.

14. Kristiane Frank, 'Blow, Detmar Jellings', in Andreas Beyer, Bénédicte Savoy and Wolf Tegethoff (eds.), *Allgemeines Künstlerlexikon – Internationale Künstlerdatenbank*, 2009.

15. For understanding this context see Drury, *Wandering Architects*, pp.85–108.

16. Antonio Brucculeri, 'Transfert du modèle Beaux-Arts dans le milieu londonien: autour de l'Architectural Association School (1900–1940)', *Cahiers HEnsA20*, no.4, June 2018, pp.33–9.

17. Following a debate on the future and outcomes of architectural education, the subject of the RIBA International Conference held in 1887, two members of the Architectural Association, Frank Baggallay and Walter Millard, one a medallist and the other a Royal Academy Travelling Fellow, initiated a training facility on 1 January 1888 under the title of 'the Atelier' in London's Regent Street. They stated: 'the Atelier is intended to afford facilities for pursuing architectural studies, both to those preparing to enter an architect's office as pupils, and to those already engaged as pupils or assistants, who desire to supplement the knowledge acquired in business hours'. AA Archives, Brown Books, session 1888–9. See also Alan Powers, 'Architectural Education in Britain, 1880–1914', PhD, University of Cambridge, 1982, vol.1, pp.29-30. On Richard Phené Spiers: A. Brucculeri, *L'importation à Londres du modèle «beaux-arts»*, paper read in the session *Apprendre et enseigner l'architecture dans l'espace européen du 19e siècle: confrontations, échanges et hybridations*, ATRHE International Conference, *Passages, transferts, trajectoires en éducation*, Université de Genève, 24–25 June 2019). On Harvey, see E. Thibault, 'Lawrence Harvey ou d'une langue à l'autre: la formation européenne d'un élève architecte dans la seconde moitié du XIXe siècle', in Armelle Le Goff and Christiane Demeulenaere-Douyère (eds), *Enseignants et enseignements au cœur de la transmission des savoirs*, Paris, CTHS, 2021.

18. Powers, vol.1, pp.85–118.

19. Julien Guadet, 'L'enseignement de l'architecture en France', *Architectural Review*, October 1903, pp 136–43; also Guadet, *Éléments et théorie de l'architecture*, 4 vols [1901–4].

20. *Architectural Review*, December 1904, pp.255–8; and September 1904, pp.110–4.

21. During the second half of the nineteenth century, only three architects with a Beaux-Arts background had received this award since its creation in 1848: Jean-Baptiste Lesueur in 1861, Jean-Louis Duc in 1876 and Charles Garnier in 1886. However, just ten years after Defrasse and

Pascal, Henri-Paul Nénot (1917) and Charles Girault (1920) also were honoured with the Gold Medal.

22. Henry Philip Cart de Lafontaine, 'Some Notes from a Parisian Atelier', *AA Journal*, vol. XXIII, no.259, September 1908, pp.240–3; 'Further Notes from a Parisian Atelier. The Entrance Examination of the École des Beaux-Arts'. *ibid.*, vol.XXIV, no.273, November 1909, pp.302–8; 'Training of the Architect in France', *ibid.*, vol.XXIX, no.319, July 1913, pp.26–8; and H.P. Cart de Lafontaine and W.R. Cable, 'The National School of Architecture', *ibid.*, vols. XXVII–XXVIII, no.316, April 1913, pp.304–6 and vol.XXIX, no.322, October 1913, pp.92–5.

23. See his personal file as a pupil of the Ecole des Beaux-Arts: Archives Nationales (Pierrefitte-sur-Seine), AJ/52/434. See also Crosnier-Leconte; and Chafee, vol.1, pp.246–8, 276–80, 406–12.

24. Powers, vol.1, pp.210–47. See also Louise Campbell, 'A Call to Order: The *Rome Prize* and Early Twentieth-Century British Architecture, *Architectural History*, vol.32, 1989, pp.131–51.

25. 'Exhibition of M. Hulot's Prix de Rome Drawings', *Journal of the RIBA*, vol.XV (third series), 23 May 1908, p.449, and R. Phené Spiers, 'M. Jean Hulot's Prix de Rome Work', *ibid.*, 25 July 1908, pp.531–2.

26. *Journal of the Royal Institute of British Architects*, 29 March 1913, p.339.

27. See the list in Chafee, vol.1, pp.307–12.

28. In chronological order: Francis Swales (Atelier Pascal), Alexander Frederick B. Anderson (Atelier Redon), Howard Robertson (Atelier Duquesne & Recoura), Eric English (Atelier Pascal), Alfred Godfrey Koerner (Atelier Lambert), Robert William Cable (Atelier Bernier), Louis de Soissons (Atelier Pascal and Recoura) and Philip Dalton Hepworth (Atelier Hébrard and Jaussely). This number seems small compared to the numbers of other groups of foreigners enrolled at the Ecole at the same time, such as Americans, Swiss and Romanians.

29. On teaching in the Beaux-Arts ateliers, see Guy Lambert, 'La pédagogie de l'atelier dans l'enseignement de l'architecture en France aux XIXe et XXe siècles, une approche culturelle et matérielle', *Perspective. Actualité en histoire de l'art*, no.1,2014, pp.129–36.

30. Fernand Billerey, 'French Modern Architecture', *Journal of the Royal Institute of British Architects,* 29 March 1913, p.320.

31 RIBA Archives, Society of Architects Papers, Council and Committees Minutes, SA-1-2-7 and Beaux-Arts Committee Minutes, SA-1-10-1. See also Powers, vol.1, pp.223–30.

32. On 5 September 1912 the Council of the Society of Architects voted to set up the Beaux-Arts Committee; on 3 October the first meeting of this committee took place and on 7 November the first draft of the workshop project was outlined. See Beaux-Arts Committee Minutes cited above, vol.1, pp.1–7. See also 'The Society of Architects Council Meeting – Interim Report of special committee in architectural training, 14 November 1912', *ibid.*, pp.3–5, the draft organization chart of the atelier (31 December 1912), p.8 and the leaflets attached to the minutes of 21 January and 9 December 1913, pp.31 and 106.

33. On the British side, one of the members of the Beaux-Arts Committee, Bartle Cox, a former student of the Laloux atelier, was in charge of the relay. Beaux-Arts Committee Minutes, 8 January, 22 May and 9 December 1913, pp.22, 65, and 106.

34. Especially in the division of competitions into *esquisses/esquisses* and *esquisses/projets rendus*, as the students' timetables show. See for example the schedule of 'esquisses-esquisses' [sic] in the 'atelier programme to January 1914' attached to the minutes of the Beaux-Arts Committee meeting of 23 October 1913, p.88. For a retrospective account of the diffusion of similar terms related to Beaux-Arts education, see Harry Stuart Goodhart-Rendel, 'Architectural Memories', *The Builder*, 16 December 1955, p.1046.

35. The aim was to exhibit them and to produce photographic directories for printing, as evidenced by the debate within the Beaux-Arts Committee about the proposal of the editor of

the *Academy Architecture* collection, Alexander Koch, to publish collections of the best work from various London establishments, following the example of those published each year by Vincent, Fréal et Cie for the Ecole des Beaux-Arts in Paris: Beaux-Arts Committee Minutes, 10 November 1915, vol.1, p.271.

36. *AA Journal,* May 1911, pp.127–8; December 1912, pp.197–8 (with an interview with SADG President A. Defrasse); June 1913, pp.16–17; and May 1920, pp.298–9. After the war, the Beaux-Arts Committee also launched the project of an exhibition of drawings by students of the Ecole des Beaux-Arts: Beaux-Arts Committee Minutes, 18 August 1919, vol.1, pp.353–4. A copy of the 1913 catalogue is in the collections of the National Art Library (V&A): *Exhibition of French Architectural Drawings*, London, Architectural Association, 1913, 46 pp.

37. See Archives nationales (Pierrefitte-sur-Seine), CP/F/12/4446/F/2, Pièce 1, *Exposition universelle de 1900. Palais des Congrès et de l'Économie sociale. Front on the Seine*; also CP/F/12/4445/E/5A and 5B, for other projects by Mewès for the Paris International Exhibition of 1900.

38. For the plan of this building see *Builders' Journal and Architectural Engineer*, 5 May 1903, p.433.

39. On Polesden Lacey, see *Architectural Review*, vol.51,1922, pp.202–7; and Robin Fedden, *Country Life*, 5 March 1948, pp.478–81 and 12 March 1948, pp.526–9.

40. See the elevation project for the expansion of headquarters of the Crédit Foncier de France in Paris, and drawing of the front door on the street, both by Charles Mewès, Drouot sales catalogue, Paris, 22 January 2021.

41. For the Hyde Park Hotel, altered by Mewès & Davis in 1901–2 and enlarged by them in 1911–12, see *Survey of London*, vol.45, 2000, pp.58–9 and Plate 33. For the Ritz, see e.g. *Modern Building Record*, vol.1, 1910, pp.166–9.

42. *Modern Building Record*, vol.2, 1911, pp.56–71.

43. *Ibid.,* vol.1, 1910, pp.16–19.

44. For this partnership see 'The Work of Mr Detmar Blow and Mr Fernand Billerey', Architectural Supplement to *Country Life*, 26 October 191), pp.v–xxxvi. As reported by Drury, p.234, 'The drawings from the Blow and Billery partnership are now lodged in the British Architectural Library, Drawings Collection … The size of the practice's output is confirmed by an index prepared by Billerey which numbers 85 significant projects undertaken with Blow up to 1920. Few relate to Blow's work prior to the formation of the partnership in 1906'.

45. For Blow and Billerey's interior work at 10 Carlton House Terrace, London, for Matthew White Ridley, 2nd Viscount Ridley, see the longitudinal section, RIBA Drawings Collection,126001, and the view of the ballroom reproduced in *The Builder*, 6 October 1911, p.391. The text in *The Builder* states that 'the main walls and general distribution of the first floor were retained, the former inside arrangement of areas, service stairs, lift wells, etc., was swept away, and the old staircase pulled down in order to build a new staircase of architectural proportions and to simplify the planning of the drawing rooms'. For the reconstruction of the Avenue (formerly Playhouse) Theatre: *Architectural Review*, January 1906, pp.36–8.

46. This façade is described in *Survey of London*, vol.40,1980, pp.252–6: '[The façade] is a fine piece of Beaux-Arts classicism, fifteen bays wide and four storeys high. The composition is tied together by a prominent modillion cornice at attic level, the balustrades below the first-floor windows and along the parapet, and the French-style channelling of the Portland stone masonry. The centrepiece is an attached Ionic portico with fluted columns stretched over three storeys. Perhaps because it is solidly executed in stone and because it is so carefully academic … the block looks more like a public building transplanted from Paris than a group of houses in Mayfair'.

47. Billerey, 'French Modern Architecture', p.330.

48. While at the Ecole des Beaux-Arts, Lawrence Harvey sent four letters to *The Builder* on the topic of French architecture and teaching: 22 January 1870, p.61; 26 February 1870, p.163; 9 April 1870, p.280; and 11 June 1870, pp.465–6. A later contribution (28 October 1871, pp.846–7) includes a section and perspective of

the new Paris Opéra. On the correspondence between Harvey and his brother concerning the writing of these articles, see E. Thibault, 'Lawrence Harvey and the architectural training in Europe', in Fernando Aliata and Eduardo Gentile (eds.), *El modelo Beaux-Arts y la arquitectura en América Latina, 1870–1930. Transferencias, intercambios y perspectivas*, Universidad Nacional de La Plata, Facultad de Arquitectura y Urbanismo, 2022, pp.165–82.

49. Fernand Billerey, 'French Modern Architecture', p.331.

50. *Ibid.*, p.335.

51. *Ibid.*, p.336.

52. *Ibid.*

53. *Journal of the Royal Institute of British Architects*, 29 March 1913, p.341.

54. 'The Patrons, Mr. Charles Mewès, Mr. Arthur Davis, and Mr. J. P. C. Chaurès, are all Beaux-Arts men, but no attempt is made to introduce French designs or details. On the contrary, the student is encouraged to develop his own ideas with the help and cooperation of the Patrons and Ateliers comrades, who assist him to lift work to the highest possible level.' RIBA Archives, Beaux-Arts Committee Minutes, vol.1, p.106.

55. See Powers, vol.1, p.104, and the letter by Charles Reilly to Blomfield (14 January 1910), quoted on pp.213–5.

56. *Journal of the Royal Institute of British Architects*, 29 March 1913, p.339.

57. To gauge the roots of this attention to the vernacular architecture of the Cotswolds, see Drury, pp.62–84.

58. On the last period of the Blow's career see Drury, pp.233–58.

59. *Journal of the Royal Institute of British Architects*, 29 March 1913, pp.340–1.

60. See the design for an armchair (a 'marquise') in the Louis XV style by Mewès and Davis, *c.*1910, Victoria & Albert Museum, Prints and Drawings, E.865:10-1975.

61. See the catalogue *Exposition anglo-française d'architecture ancienne & moderne, mai 1914, organisée par la Société des architectes diplômés par le gouvernement*, Paris, SADG, 1914. Another exhibition on decorative arts in Britain was opened at the same time in Paris. See *Arts décoratifs de Grande-Bretagne et d'Irlande: Palais du Louvre, pavillon de Marsan, avril-octobre 1914, exposition organisée par le Gouvernement britannique*, London, 1914. There were several Franco-British exhibitions during the period 1904–14, notably the privately sponsored exhibition held in London at 'White City' in 1908. See Alexander C.T. Geppert, *Fleeting Cities: Imperial Expositions in Fin-de-Siècle Europe*, 2010, pp.101–33.

62. In opposition to the repertoire of nineteenth-century historicist architecture and the spread of neo-Gothic in England, Blomfield alludes to Decimus Burton, John Soane, George Basevi, Charles Robert Cockerell, and 'the compromise' of Charles Barry for his project for the Houses of Parliament ('elsewhere he invariably adhered to his rather florid Classic') as representatives of English classical tradition. See R. Blomfield, *Preface*, in *Exposition anglo-française d'architecture*, p.7.

63. *Ibid.*, Section XV, *Travaux des élèves de l'Ecole supérieure des beaux-arts de Paris*, pp.51–2.

10 · Contributors

ANTONIO BRUCCULERI graduated from the Università Iuav di Venezia, where his doctoral thesis was on Louis Hautecœur, published by Picard (Paris, 2007). He specializes in architectural and urban history from the end of the eighteenth to the early years of the twentieth centuries. He lectured at the Ecole Pratique des Hautes Etudes (2009–14) and is currently professor at ENSA (Paris-La Villette), researcher at the Laboratoire AHTTEP/UMR AUSser and an associate researcher at HISTARA (EPHE) and EVCAU (ENSA Paris-Val de Seine).

ALEXANDRINA BUCHANAN is Reader in Archive Studies at the University of Liverpool. Author of *Robert Willis and the Foundation of Architectural History* (2013) and co-author of *Digital Analysis of Vaults in English Medieval Architecture* (2021), her research explores both medieval and revival architecture, with a particular interest in historiography and the interplay between knowledge and design.

HOWARD COUTTS has been a curator at the Bowes Museum since 1990. He took his degree in History and History of Art at Cambridge in 1978, before joining the V&A in what is now the 'Word and Image' department where he worked with architectural drawing and other designs. He has produced one book on the history of ceramic design 1500–1830 and numerous exhibition catalogues and entries devoted to fine and decorative arts 1400–1900.

JAMES EDGAR has been studying and practising historic buildings conservation for more than forty years, working first in Scotland and then in England before becoming a statutory officer for English Heritage in Central London. A subsequent spell in the East Midlands focussed on the only compulsory purchase case ever undertaken by the Secretary of State: Apethorpe Hall. In recent years he has been on his own, providing services for a wide range of clients. One of them bought John Corbett's house at Impney and his hotel in nearby Droitwich.

MICHAEL HALL is the Editor of *The Burlington Magazine*. He is the author of *Waddesdon Manor: The Biography of a Rothschild House* (third edition, 2009).

PETER HOWELL is a classicist and former Chairman of the Victorian Society. He recently published *John Francis Bentley* and *The Triumphal Arch*.

GILLES MAURY is an architect, Ph. D. in architectural history since 2009. He is a lecturer at ENSAP Lille. He is currently preparing an HDR on *Viollet-le-Duc and England, research and exchanges on housing and modern Gothic*. He specialises in 19th century architecture and international exchanges.

ANDREW SAINT is a long-time member of the Victorian Society, currently chairs the Society's Publications Committee and has been a member of the Southern Buildings Committee for many years. He was General Editor of the Survey of London between 2006 and 2015. He has written a number of books, most recently *London 1870–1914: A City at its Zenith*.

JOSEPH SPECKLIN was born in Mulhouse. In 2004, he achieved a Master in *Histoire contemporaine* (Late Modern History) at the Université de Haute-Alsace with a Master's thesis about the three places of worship designed by the architect Jean-Baptiste Schacre (1808–76) in Mulhouse. In 2008, he was the curator of an exhibition commemorating the bicentenary of Schacre's birth (Musée Historique de Mulhouse). He's a certified teacher in History, Geography and Art History. Since 2007, he's been teaching at the Collège J.-J. Souhait at Saint-Dié-des-Vosges.